LIBERATION THEOLOGY

Also by Phillip Berryman

Inside Central America: The Essential Facts Past and Present on El Salvador, Nicaragua, Honduras, Guatemala, and Costa Rica

The Religious Roots of Rebellion: Christians in Central American Revolutions

LIBERATION THEOLOGY

ESSENTIAL FACTS ABOUT THE REVOLUTIONARY MOVEMENT IN LATIN AMERICA—AND BEYOND

PHILLIP BERRYMAN

TEMPLE UNIVERSITY PRESS
PHILADELPHIA

 Published in the United States by Temple University Press, Philadelphia 19122. Published by arrangement with Pantheon Books, a division of Random House, Inc., New York.

Library of Congress Catalog Card No. 86-051399

ISBN 0-87722-479-X

Book design by Guenet Abraham

Manufactured in the United States of America

CONTENTS

INTRODUCTION

ON SUNDAY MORNING, MARCH 23, 1980, I WAS IN THE crowded church in San Salvador where Archbishop Oscar Romero was preaching. Poor people, elbow to elbow, overflowed from the aisles in the late morning heat. For over an hour Romero wove a commentary on the scriptural passages for the day, the fourth Sunday in Lent, around the theme of liberation in one's own person, in the community, and in relation to God.

Romero's voice was being transmitted through the countryside for the first time in weeks, after bomb damage to the archdiocesan radio station had been repaired. During the last part of the sermon Romero commented briefly on many events of the previous week that the media would not report or would cover only in distorted versions. The National Guard was accusing Father Ricardo Ayala of being involved with guerrillas;

the police had made a search of a parish house of some Belgian priests; the archdiocese was opening facilities to take in refugees fleeing violence in the countryside; troops had surrounded the national university for a whole day; other troops had stormed the Catholic university and killed a student; throughout the week many people had been arrested unjustly. Amnesty International had found some 83 people had been killed between March 10 and 14. (Although guerrilla war was not to break out for many months, the church later documented 588 killings during this month, almost all the work of government and right-wing forces.)

Romero ended with a plea to members of the army and the security forces not to kill the peasants.

> My brothers, they are part of our very own people. You are killing your own fellow peasants. God's law, "Thou shalt not kill!" takes precedence over a human being's order to kill. No soldier is obliged to obey an order that is against God's law. No one has to obey an immoral law.

He continued pleading with them—even ordering them—to stop the repression.

After the mass I was talking with a theologian who was close to Romero. When I expressed my concern about such a direct challenge to the military, he said the matter had been discussed during the regular Saturday afternoon meeting of a team of priests, sisters, and lay people with whom Romero consulted for his sermons. The team had agreed that the level of killing made it necessary despite the risk.

I was in El Salvador with an ecumenical church group. After the mass we attended a press conference, then met with Romero and some of his advisors. With his crew cut and glasses, and his clerical demeanor, Romero did not fit my idea of a prophet. Later in the afternoon we interviewed some of the first refugees of the conflict, whom he had received on the grounds of the seminary where the archdiocesan offices were also located. Late that night, as I was walking down a deserted avenue in San Salvador, I began to wonder whether this sermon might not seal Romero's fate.

The next day in the street we found a mimeographed hate sheet comparing Romero to Khomeini. On Monday evening, as we were interviewing the Salvadoran Human Rights Commission, word arrived that Romero had been shot while saying mass. We spent the next two days in the company of his stunned and grief-stricken coworkers; the funeral itself was disrupted by a bomb and automatic weapon attack.

Those moments—that sermon, Romero's murder, his funeral—are among the most important in my life. They also express the core of liberation theology. What the archbishop said had an undeniable political impact—he was telling soldiers to disobey. Yet he was simply reminding them of God's command "Thou shalt not kill!" His aim in preaching was to point to the genuine theological sense of the pain and struggle in El Salvador, and to enable people to continue hoping. Out of a similar kind of faith many Latin Americans have risked and sacrificed their lives.

Liberation theology has attracted considerable attention in recent years. On each of Pope John Paul II's major trips to Latin America (Mexico, 1979; Brazil, 1980; Central America, 1983; Andean countries of South America, 1985), he has issued warnings apparently aimed at theologians. In September 1984 the Vatican published a major document pointing to its dangers, and in 1985 it silenced the Brazilian Franciscan priest Leonardo Boff. In Nicaragua priests serve in a revolutionary government, while the Catholic bishops are leading opposition figures.

The controversy is not a purely internal church matter; it has played a major role in the Reagan administration's efforts to justify its Central American policy. A 1980 document blueprinting a new policy on Latin America, written by the Committee of Santa Fe, whose members were part of the Reagan circle, stated that "U.S. policy must begin to counter (not react against) liberation theology as it is utilized in Latin America by the 'liberation theology' clergy."

Journalistic accounts all too easily reinforce simplistic stereotypes, portraying liberation theology as an exotic brew of Marxism and Christianity, or as a movement of rebel priests bent on challenging church authority. The aim of this book is quite simply to get beyond the clichés and to explain what liberation theology is (primarily in Latin America), how it arose, how it works in practice, and its implications. Some initial observations may be helpful for beginning the discussion.

Liberation theology is theology—that is, it is a systematic, disciplined reflection on Christian faith and its implications. Its proponents were trained as theologians, usually in Europe, and they write about the same topics that Christian theologians have always taken up: God, creation, Jesus Christ, the church, grace, and so forth. This point is not always self-evident. The Santa Fe Committee accuses liberation theologians of using the church "as a political weapon against private property and productive capitalism by infiltrating the religious community with ideas that are less Christian than Communist."

Readers will be able to judge for themselves whether that accusation is accurate or fair. At this point I would simply assert that one cannot understand liberation theology unless one sees it as theology.

Unlike their colleagues in other parts of the world, these theologians generally do not teach in universities and seminaries, at least not full-time. They are a relatively small group. Those who have published significant works number about two or three dozen. They are almost all male, and most are Catholic clerics, although Protestants have played important roles in the movement. These theologians often serve as advisors to grassroots groups and to priests, sisters, and pastors working with grass-roots groups. Most of them spend some of their time working directly with the poor themselves. The questions they deal with are those that arise out of this contact with the poor.

In fact, liberation theology is an interpretation of Christian faith out of the experience of the poor. It is an attempt to read the Bible and key Christian doctrines with the eyes of the poor.

It is at the same time an attempt to help the poor interpret their own faith in a new way. To take a simple but central example, in traditional Latin American piety Jesus is almost mute, indeed most often represented dead on the cross. Perhaps the fact that their society crucifies them and keeps them mute makes ordinary Latin Americans identify with such a Christ. Liberation theology focuses on Jesus' life and message. For example, in his initial sermon, a kind of manifesto, Jesus quotes Isaiah, "He has sent me to bring glad tidings to the poor, to proclaim liberty to captives . . ." and says that the passage is fulfilled in him. The poor learn to read the Scripture in a way that affirms their dignity and self-worth and their right to struggle together for a more decent life.

People do not simply happen to be poor; their poverty is largely a product of the way society is organized. Hence, liberation theology is a critique of economic structures that enable some Latin Americans to jet to Miami or London to shop, while most of their fellow citizens do not have safe drinking water. In particular, liberation theologians have critiqued the ideologies that justify such inequality, including their use of religious symbols. Military dictatorships have often practiced torture to defend what they are fond of calling "Western 'Christian' civilization."

A further area of questioning has been the activity of the church and of Christians. By what criterion should the church organize its pastoral work? Take, for example, the question of church unity. As the level of social conflict increases and societies become polarized, Christians find themselves on opposing sides. Unity, however, is supposed to be one of the distinguishing features of Christianity. What should be the criterion for such unity? Obedience to the bishops and the pope? Is division in the church to be avoided at all cost? Liberation theology seeks to respond to questions and seeming dilemmas that arise out of the experience of the church, often in conflictive situations.

As an initial description, we may say that liberation theology is

1. An interpretation of Christian faith out of the suffering, struggle, and hope of the poor.
2. A critique of society and the ideologies sustaining it.
3. A critique of the activity of the church and of Christians from the angle of the poor.

This is at once a new interpretation of the meaning of Christianity and the recovery of a prophetic tradition present in the Bible itself. That tradition has periodically recurred within the history of Christianity, although it is usually suppressed as heresy.

Liberation theology is not unique to Latin America: there are new Asian and African Christian theologies, as well as feministic theology and black theology. The poor, nonwhites, and women are finding new meaning in Christian faith as well as revealing the shortcomings of interpretations made by white Western males.

The shift underway may turn out to be as significant as the Protestant Reformation, which began as a revolt against corrupt practices in the Roman church, and quickly became a new Bible-based theology and a new model of church. With their stress on personal conversion and conviction, the Reformation churches were more in tune with the modern age than Roman Catholicism, and indeed they helped shape that age. What began as a religious movement had a profound impact on subsequent history. It is conceivable that liberation theology represents the initial phase of a comparable shift in the history of Christianity and that its impact will go far beyond the churches.

Liberation theology is also one manifestation of a worldwide movement for human emancipation. That may sound almost archaic in the United States and Western Europe in the mid-1980s, when journalists are fond of seeing any political activism as a throwback to the 1960s and in particular to uprisings in the United States. Yet surely the twentieth century will turn out to be more than the "American century." When the history of our age is written—perhaps by a nonwhite hand—it may also be the story of the emergence onto the stage of history of the poor majority of the human family.

It could be argued that one cannot understand Latin America today without understanding what liberation theology represents. The fates of North America and Latin America are increasingly interconnected; just consider the Latin American debt. Few have noticed that of the twelve hundred delegates to a conference on the debt held in Havana in August 1985 over one hundred were Catholic priests. In his closing address Premier Fidel Castro read a letter from Cardinal Paulo Evaristo Arns of São Paulo, Brazil, to the conference, stating that the debt should not be paid at the cost of the poor. The delegates gave a prolonged standing ovation. As the debt crisis deepens, will liberation theology be a factor leading the church to take a prominent role?

A person seeking to understand liberation theology can already find a number of translations and surveys in English. Virtually all of them, however, are published by church-related presses and are directed primarily to a church public. What I have attempted here is to make this movement intelligible to a general public, drawing on twenty years of my own experience. While serving as a Catholic priest in a barrio in Panama City in the 1960s, I went to South America to seek out Latin American theologians. Although I resigned from the priesthood in 1973, my work, especially as American Friends Service Committee representative in Central America from 1976 to 1980, has kept me close to the Latin American church. What I have learned there, the ideas of the theologians as well as commitment like Archbishop Romero's, has been a kind of compass for my own life, however errantly I may follow it.

A reader who casually picks up the writings of liberation theologians might be surprised at the seemingly abstract tone. As much as the theologians insist on the primacy of "praxis," they do not devote much attention to specific experiences and events. They seem to assume that their readers—Latin Americans—do not need to be reminded of local and specific realities. In this book I have tried to root liberation theology in events, and to show its practical impact at the village and barrio level. Nevertheless, my aim is not to tell the story of the churches in Latin America—that can already be found in many fine recent works—but to explain as clearly as possible the ideas of liberation theologians.

I have been struck by the divergence between North American assumptions and Latin American questions. For example, almost any lecture on liberation theology in the United States or Europe will elicit questions on violence and on Marxism. Yet the theologians have very little—practically nothing—to say on violence and devote surprisingly little attention to discussion of Marxism. On the other hand, they spend a great deal of time on seemingly ethereal questions such as the relationship between the kingdom of God and efforts to achieve human dignity here and now. I have tried to center this presentation on what the liberation theologians consider important, while at the same time remaining sensitive to the questions of audiences in the more developed countries of the West.

Chapter One describes the overall context of the 1960s and the initial proposals of the theologians. Chapters Two through Four focus on how liberation theology functions at the village or barrio level. In Chapter Five I make some observations on the theologians' overall enterprise. Chapter Six then describes the changing context from the early 1970s to the present. There follow several chapters on particular topics, especially those related to liberation theology's political impact. Chapter Eleven surveys Third World, black, Hispanic, and feminist theologies. Chapter Twelve discusses the major objections posed by critics. The book closes with a tentative assessment of liberation theology and its future.

1. BIRTH PANGS

Emergence of Liberation Theology

AT THE HEART OF ANY CITY OR TOWN IN LATIN AMERICA IS a plaza. Along one side stands a cathedral, church, or chapel and along another side the presidential palace, city hall, or other official building. The architectural embodiments of the religious and civil powers face each other across the center of inhabited space.

From its first appearance in the New World, the Catholic church was part of the overall enterprise of conquest and colonization of the native peoples by Spain and Portugal and the imposition of colonial rule. Pope Alexander VI adjudicated the division of the new continent between Spain and Portugal and conferred on their monarchies the right and duty of propagating the Catholic faith. Moreover, the conquest brought a particularly aggressive kind of Catholicism, reflecting both the period in which Spain defeated the Moors, and Catholicism's vigorous reaction to the Protestant Reformation.

Some of the early missionaries, however, protested the cruelty of the conquest. The most well known is Bartolomé de las Casas, who came to Hispaniola in 1502 (his father and brothers had been part of Columbus' second voyage). Las Casas became a Dominican priest in 1512. Although he himself had held Indian slaves, las Casas experienced a conversion reading the book of Sirach, including this verse: "He slays his neighbor who deprives him of his living: he sheds blood who denies the laborer his wages" (34:22). He went on to devote his life to struggling on behalf of the Indians. Las Casas argued that the Indians were better off as living pagans than as dead Christians, and insisted that they must be won over by the power of the gospel rather than the force of arms. Well over a dozen of the bishops in the sixteenth century, mainly Dominicans, were outstanding in their defense of the Indians. The bishop of Nicaragua, Antonio de Valdivieso, was even stabbed to death in 1550 by one of the governor's henchmen. Today's liberation theologians regard this early generation of bishops as their precursors. They were exceptions, however.

The model of social order the Iberian conquerors brought was that of "christendom." Since the fall of the Roman Empire European society had been ruled by a kind of dual power, civil and ecclesiastical. The church could count on the backing of civil authority, and the civil authority was seen as rooted in a superior order that reached up to the very throne of God. Relations were not always harmonious, but the overall pattern was that of a single "Christian" society where civil and religious authority were closely connected. This model arrived in Latin America just as it was beginning to unravel in Europe, starting with the Protestant Reformation. The Latin American form aptly can be called "colonial christendom."

Since monasteries, convents, and churches were located in the towns, the poor in the outlying areas had only occasional contact with the church's official representatives. To a great extent they accepted Catholicism on their own terms. Their religion, with its own prayers and devotions, its own concerns and interests, its own center of gravity and worldview—what scholars would later call "popular Catholicism"—was transmitted more through family and village than through the official church.

During the years 1808 to 1824 Latin America broke away from Spain and Portugal. The independence movement was largely the work of the local elites, who were motivated not only by nationalism but by a desire to be free to trade directly with the new center of world power, Great Britain. The poor served in the armies that struggled for independence, but they reaped little benefit. They remained under the domination of the local landholding and commercial classes. Although Latin American countries have been formally independent since the early nineteenth century, today many regard full nationhood as unfinished business.

For the Catholic church the independence struggle and its aftermath meant a severe crisis. The bishops tended to side with the Spanish Crown, and popes made pronouncements against the independence struggle in 1816 and 1823. Many clerics, on the other hand, supported independence (for example, the well-known Mexican priests Hidalgo and Morelos).

Nevertheless, independence led to institutional crisis. The Vatican only began to recognize the new states in 1831, and many bishops departed, leaving some dioceses vacant. The church became tied to so-called Conservative parties that battled parties designated "Liberal" in almost all countries. The Liberals viewed themselves as the party of progress and development, especially by expanding export agriculture. They found it convenient to pass laws that would enable them to confiscate land from Catholic religious orders and Indians. To their "progressive" eyes, these were backward or obscurantist elements.

As a result of independence and attacks from Liberal governments, the Catholic church was thrust into a situation of chronic weakness and crisis. One consequence is that most Latin American countries have never produced sufficient clergy and have depended on a steady flow from Europe. Today the

Catholic clergy in several countries—Guatemala, Nicaragua, Honduras, Venezuela, Panama, Bolivia—is around 80 percent foreign.

Protestant missionary efforts began during the closing decades of the last century. Liberal governments often saw Protestants as representing "modernity" and as a useful force for countering "backward" Catholicism. Evangelical missionaries often brought an amalgam of fundamentalism and U.S. cultural patterns (American hymns set to Spanish words), while those of more liberal tendencies brought the "social gospel" with American assumptions (U.S. electoral democracy). Despite impressive growth rates Protestants remained a minority, and most Latin Americans continued to see themselves as Catholic.

During the first half of the twentieth century Latin American Catholicism began to rebound. One sign was the growth of Catholic Action movements among workers and students. In 1955 bishops from all over the continent met in Rio de Janeiro for the first plenary meeting of CELAM (Latin American Bishops' Conference). Although the bishops' concerns—the spread of Protestantism, communism, and secularism—seemed defensive, they were also beginning to recognize the social problems of the continent.

Critics and New Questions

How could a theology of liberation arise from a church so historically conservative? The answer is to be found in the experience of crisis in Latin American societies starting in the 1960s and the impact of Vatican Council II and its aftermath on the Catholic church. Indeed, in Latin America, events in the church and in society as a whole are intertwined. In the 1960s new questions about the social order urgently demanded new answers, and church people felt a new freedom to respond.

Consider the situation of the typical rural parish priest. He might have twenty thousand or more parishioners living in villages scattered through the hills or fields around the main town. Most would be baptized and consider themselves Catholics, but the priest could get to their villages only at intervals of several weeks, and then his contact would be primarily for ritual events, such as the mass, baptism, or marriage. In such circumstances he could scarcely have any meaningful communication with people, let alone engage in any relevant teaching of Christianity. With the kind of theology that he had learned in the seminary, he might believe that in some mysterious way God was using his sacramental action to save people. However, the more optimistic kind of theology that was then gaining ground—that God's salvation reaches people everywhere, whether or not they are good Catholics—could not but raise questions about the significance of his own life and activity as a priest.

If he looked more closely, he could have another reason for doubts. Since he lived on the money he collected from the people, the peasants might see him as not too different from the government officials, store owners, and loan sharks in the town. His own standard of living might be modest, but it came from contributions of the poor. Institutionally, moreover, the church was disproportionately serving the privileged, since priests and sisters were concentrated in the larger cities, often in Catholic schools for the rich. To the extent he began to be socially conscious, such a priest became aware of the church's complicity with an unjust social order.

Many priests and sisters working at the local level began to raise questions about their activity. Certain political events, such as the Cuban revolution and the experience of Brazil in the early 1960s, began to raise institutional questions.

The Cuban experience was significant for what did not happen. Christians as such played no important role in the overthrow of the Batista dictatorship, and the church soon became the refuge for those Cubans who resented the implementation of revolutionary changes. Some bishops and many priests left the country, further weakening a church already institutionally feeble. The Cuban government and Communist Party took an officially atheist line. Virtually no one in the church seems to have posed in theological and pastoral terms the possibility that Christians could take a positive attitude toward the revolution. (Only in the late 1960s did some Cuban bishops begin to move toward a positive assessment of the revolution.)

Inspired by Cuba's example, rural guerrilla movements arose in Venezuela, Guatemala, Peru, and a number of other countries. In response, the Kennedy administration launched the Alliance for Progress, which combined development aid with an upgrading of armies and police to meet the threat of insurgency. A shared anxiety about revolution tended to unite church people, Christian Democratic parties, and foreign aid agencies.

What Brazilians experienced and the questions they raised in the late 1950s and early 1960s foreshadowed what was to happen in the rest of the continent. Under President Juscelino Kubitschek (1955–60), the government sought to give an impulse to economic development. The president himself used Christian language, calling social injustice, for example, "a great sin against Christ." Becoming critical of the landholding oligarchy, the Catholic hierarchy formed an alliance with the government that led to the creation of a large development agency for the rural Northeast. Nevertheless, the government acted in the technocratic top-down manner that would later receive the pejorative name "developmentalism."

On the other hand, peasant leagues were becoming militant, and radicalized middle-class people, particularly university students, were going to work directly with the poor. Paulo Freire, an educator in the Northeast, developed a new method for teaching literacy through a process of *conscientização* (consciousness-raising, see Chapter Two). Catholic Action movements of students and workers became involved as did significant Catholic intellectuals. Some Christians began to utilize Marxist concepts for analyzing society. Richard Shaull, a Presbyterian missionary, raised the question of whether revolution had a theological significance. He and young Protestants were beginning to discuss such topics with Dominican priests and Catholic intellectuals.

All this ferment led to a crisis for the church. In the prevailing view of things, the church could train people and could promote "social action," including development projects, but had no role in the realm of politics proper. This theoretically clear notion was proving increasingly unsatisfactory in practice. To the extent it became undeniable that the causes of poverty were structural and would require basic structural changes, it seemed obvious that such changes would come about only through political action. It was inconsistent to call for structural change but refuse to become politically involved. This question came up in several contexts, most notably in the movement called Ação Popular, which grew out of Catholic Action. Discussion was cut short, however, when the armed forces became alarmed by the growing grass-roots militancy and staged a coup in March 1964. Many intellectuals, politicians, and popular leaders had to flee the country, and the church was largely silenced for almost a decade.

Vatican II

In the 1950s it would have been as difficult for Catholics to imagine the pope launching a broad reform movement within the church as it would be for Americans today to conceive of the Kremlin initiating a far-reaching democratization of the Eastern bloc countries. Yet that is what occurred with the Second Vatican Council.

Roman Catholicism's very identity was anchored in unchangeability. Its response to the call of Luther and the other sixteenth-century reformers for direct access to the Bible, personal faith, and worship in the people's own language was to dig in its heels and reaffirm most of the very elements the reformers were criticizing. During the following centuries the Catholic church mistrusted science and all aspects of the modern world. Nineteenth-century popes, for example, condemned the very idea of democracy. The function of theology was not to raise new questions but to defend the Roman Catholic system. In the crisis that followed World War II European theologians began to pursue new questions with scriptural and historical studies and in dialogue with existentialism only to be stopped by Pope Pius XII's encyclical *Humani Generis* (1950).

For centuries church authorities had been piling sandbags higher and higher to withstand the rising waters of modernity. With Vatican II the dam broke.

In early 1959 John XXIII, whom many had expected to be a caretaker pope, called for the first council since Vatican Council I (1869–70), which had defined papal infallibility. In the opening days of the council in the fall of 1962, a group of European bishops thwarted efforts at control by Vatican officials and established an open atmosphere. In the council's plenary sessions and working groups, ideas and proposals that had been cautiously advanced only in progressive theological circles were legitimized. The first complete document, the decree on worship (1963), ended the Latin mass that had been the norm for fifteen centuries.

With Vatican II the Catholic church, as it were, turned itself inside out. Prior to the council Catholics were taught that their main business in life was to remain in the "state of grace" and get to heaven. The church was the custodian of the means of grace and truth. In such a scheme earthly matters were ultimately inconsequential. At Vatican II, accepting and building on decades of work by theologians, the Catholic church modestly accepted its "pilgrim" status, journeying alongside the rest of humankind. In a further radical shift the church began to see in "human progress" evidence of God's working in human history.

European and North American bishops and theologians set the agenda for Vatican II. Latin American bishops had only a modest role, as when they and other Third World bishops insisted that the document on the church in the modern world should deal with the issue of development. Priests, sisters, and lay activists in Latin America welcomed the initial results of the council, such as the shift to the vernacular language and the general liberalizing tone.

Far more important than any of its particular decisions was the fact that the council led Latin American Catholics to take a much more critical look at their own church and their own society. Not only did they seek to adopt the council to Latin America—they began to ask Latin American questions.

Camilo Torres: The Price of Commitment

When Vatican II closed in December 1965, Father Camilo Torres had already joined the Colombian guerrillas and would soon die in combat. Although very few church people joined guerrilla movements, many underwent a similar radicalization process. Torres' consistency in moving from words to action made him a kind of instant icon. He intuitively anticipated much of what was to become liberation theology.

Born into an upper-class Bogotá family, Torres studied theology and sociology in Belgium during the 1950s, and then returned to his country to work as a sociologist and university chaplain. In the early 1960s he did research in Colombia, producing studies on issues like urbanization, living standards, land reform, political violence, education, democracy, and the practice of sociology itself. Gradually, he moved away from academic sociology and into doing training courses with peasants around the country. Concluding that conventional politics, with its oligarchically controlled parties, could not bring significant change, he began to propose something that seemed eminently logical, the formation of a broadly based United Front that would link together peasants, workers, slum dwellers, professional people, and others to pressure for basic change. His good looks and earnestness and the fact that he was a priest—in the most "Catholic" country in Latin America—made him an exciting new kind of public figure. Torres spoke openly of the need for revolution, defining it as a "fundamental change in economic, social and political structures." Power had to be taken away from the privileged and given to the poor majorities—that was the essence of revolution. It could be peaceful if the privileged elites did not put up violent resistance. In language that echoed the gospels Torres said that revolution was

> the way to bring about a government that feeds the hungry, clothes the naked, teaches the ignorant, puts into practice the works of charity, and love for neighbor, not just every now and then, and not just for a few, but for the majority of our neighbors.

Christians had to become involved in revolution, since that was the only effective way to "make love for everyone a reality."

In May 1965 the United Front platform, based largely on a draft by Torres, became public. Rushing around Colombia to address crowds, Torres expressed his thinking in a series of manifestolike "messages" to different audiences: Christians, Communists, military men, trade unionists, students, peasants, and women (for a Latin American male in 1965 he had a rather clear and critical vision). Yet even as he strove to build a nationwide political movement, Torres was developing contacts with the ELN (Army of National Liberation) guerrillas. Pressured by Cardinal Luis Concha of Bogotá, he accepted laicization, although he continued to regard what he was doing as an outgrowth of his priestly calling.

The army had already detected Torres' ELN ties when he received the order to drop his political work and join the guerrillas. His short fighting career ended on February 15, 1966, when he was killed in combat.

On a conceptual level Torres' theology remained largely what he had learned in Louvain, and his sociology had only hints of what would soon become the "dependence theory." Yet in his movement from theory to practice, from analysis to involvement—to the point of sacrificing his life—and in the way he focused Christianity on effective love for neighbor, he became a paradigmatic figure for many Christians.

This does not mean that many priests rushed to join the guerrillas; only a handful have done so during the past twenty years. What struck the consciences of many Christians was Torres' willingness to follow his convictions to their ultimate consequences.

Declaring Intellectual Independence

Revolution was in the air in the mid-1960s. Even President Eduardo Frei called his Christian Democratic program in Chile a "Revolution in Liberty." The implication was that he could bring about changes in Chilean society without sacrificing "liberty." Cuba was of course the unmentioned term of comparison.

Latin American social scientists were beginning to question the possibility of genuine development within the present world order. Their ideas were popularized as the "dependence theory." Conventional ideas of development diagnosed underdevelopment as "backwardness," and assumed that development could be achieved by following the path already traced out by the "advanced" countries. After examining their own history, however, Latin Americans were concluding that all their development—from conquest to the present—had been the result of events in Europe, and later in North America. Their whole history could be written around successive exports (gold and silver, dyes, hides, rubber, coffee, and so forth) exploited by the centers of world production and their local allies, the landholding classes. Their twentieth-century industry was not their own but that of giant foreign corporations. Underdevelopment was structural. The most apt terms were not "advanced" and "backward" but "dominant" and "dependent." Striving to "catch up" would be in vain; their only hope was to break the chains of dependence (see Chapters Five and Twelve for further discussion of Latin American social theory).

Whatever its merits, dependence theory was more than a new idea—it was a new paradigm applicable not only in economics but in the social and human sciences generally. In its original form it was developed largely by Latin Americans as a kind of declaration of cultural and intellectual independence. It is worth noting that the 1960s also saw the emergence of a generation of superb Latin American novelists, such as Gabriel García Márquez, Julio Cortázar, and Mario Vargas Llosa. The new pastoral and theological approaches took form at a moment when Latin America was affirming its own identity.

Vatican II encouraged church people to enter into dialogue with "the world." Viewed optimistically from Europe, that world seemed to be one of rapid technological and social change. A Third World angle of vision, however, revealed a world of vast poverty and oppression that seemed to call for revolution. Several documents in the postcouncil period reinforced that impression.

One key document was Pope Paul VI's 1967 encyclical *Populorum Progressio* (On the Progress of Peoples). Contrary to his predecessors, whose documents on Catholic "social teaching" reflected European preoccupations, Paul VI focused on Third World development issues. Within its generally moderate tone the encyclical hinted at a strong critique of the existing international economic order. The *Wall Street Journal* called it "warmed-over Marxism." Nevertheless, the pope seemed to assume that development would be achieved through consensus rather than struggle. In Latin America the most quoted passage was paragraph 31:

> We know . . . that a revolutionary uprising—save where there is manifest long-standing tyranny which would do great damage to fundamental personal rights and dangerous harm to the com-

> mon good of the country—produces new injustices, throws more elements out of balance and brings on new disasters.

Shortly afterward, a group of eighteen Third World bishops, half from Brazil, drew up a statement that went considerably further than the pope's, while quoting him abundantly. They took a positive view of revolution and approvingly quoted the statement of a bishop during Vatican II: "Authentic socialism is Christianity lived to the full, in basic equality and with a fair distribution of goods."

In Argentina a group of priests in turn used this statement of the "Bishops of the Third World" as its own starting point and called itself the Movement of Priests for the Third World. Similar priest groups sprang up in Peru, Colombia, Mexico, and elsewhere. They became the most ardent articulators of a new sense of crisis, possibly because they had to deal with the disparity between the new ideals emerging from the council and the everyday reality they experienced. In a flurry of manifestos such groups raised questions about the role of the church. Did Catholicism reinforce fatalism, acting as an "opiate"? Should the church sell its properties? Should not priests give up their privileges and live like ordinary people? They also critiqued existing society. Implicitly responding to the pope's warning against violence, one document pointed to a "centuries-old pattern of violence that has been produced by the existing economic, political, social and cultural power structures." Sisters were also beginning to question traditional kinds of work, such as teaching in private schools, and to move toward pastoral work with the poor, but they did not take public stands.

By no means did all, or even a majority, of priests and sisters become radicalized. At its height the Third World Movement included eight hundred of Argentina's five thousand priests as its members, and the proportion in other countries was no doubt less. Nevertheless, this radicalized clergy played a role out of proportion to its numbers, particularly since they were in more direct contact with poor sectors of the population, while much of the rest of the clergy was working in schools.

Throughout this period Protestant pastors and theologians were raising similar questions.

Medellín—the Magna Carta

In August 1968 about 130 Catholic bishops (representing more than 600 in Latin America) met in Medellín, Colombia, for the task of applying Vatican II to Latin America. It was the high-water mark of worldwide upheaval of the 1960s. Students had occupied universities throughout the United States, and Chicago police had beaten protestors at the Democratic convention; striking factory workers had linked up with students in the Paris May, momentarily seeming to threaten the prevailing order; the Soviet Union had invaded Czechoslovakia and ended the "Prague spring"; Mexican police had fired on demonstrators at the Plaza of Tlatelolco, killing an estimated four hundred. Pope Paul VI's 1967 reaffirmation of the church's ban on contraception, contrary to the recommendation of an expert commission he himself had appointed, had accelerated a growing authority crisis within the Catholic church itself.

The Medellín meeting was the second plenary meeting of CELAM (Latin American Bishops' Conference); the first had been held in Rio de Janeiro in 1955. In preparation for the meeting the CELAM staff had circulated among the bishops a preparatory document that surveyed economic conditions, living standards, the cultural situation, and political life in terms not very different from some of the manifestos mentioned above. It then went on to consider the presence of the church in society, and closed with several pages of theological reflection.

That procedure itself—to start with observations on society and then take up the church—was a break from the traditional from-doctrine-to-application mode which insinuates that truth comes down to earth from above. In their discussions and the documents they produced, the bishops first assessed the overall situation and only then moved to brief theological reflections, and finally urged pastoral commitments. This three-part structure was apparent not only in each individual document but in the structure of the published conclusions. The more secular topics (justice, peace, education, family, youth) preceded the more church-related ones (pastoral work, priests, religious, lay people, church structures, and so forth).

In ringing phrases the bishops called for Christians to be involved in the transformation of society. They denounced "institutionalized violence" and referred to it as a "situation of sin" (thus expanding the traditional notion of sin focused on individual transgressions of a divine law); they called for "sweeping, bold, urgent, and profoundly renovating changes"; they described education as a process that could enable people "to become agents of their own advancement." At one point the bishops compared three types of mind-sets. "Revolutionaries" were described more favorably than "traditionalists" or "developmentalists" (who were viewed as technocrats). Revolutionaries were defined as those seeking radical change and who believed that the people should chart their own course—not as those using violence. Pastorally, the bishops spelled out a number of commitments, such as defending human rights and carrying out a "consciousness-raising evangelization." They committed the church to share the condition of the poor out of solidarity. In several places the documents spoke of *comunidades de base,* "base communities," a term that had recently been coined to denote small, lay-led groups of Christians. Few such communities existed then, but they would soon become very widespread.

The bishops frequently used "liberation" and similar terms, and they explicitly likened "genuine development," the "transition from less human to more human conditions for each and every person" to the biblical exodus.

The Medellín documents also left a good deal of ambiguity. The terminologies of development and liberation were intertwined, and the underlying assumption seemed to be that basic change could come through a conversion on the part of the privileged and powerful. There was no strong endorsement of the right of the oppressed to struggle for their rights, perhaps because the bishops feared they would be interpreted as endorsing violence. That the documents were as strong as they were reflected the input of a minority of bishops and a solid group of a hundred expert advisors, who undoubtedly did most of the drafting.

Priests, sisters, and lay activists eagerly seized the Medellín documents as a Magna Carta justifying a whole new pastoral approach.

Liberation Theology—First Maps

One of the advisors at Medellín was the Peruvian theologian Gustavo Gutiérrez, whose hand can be seen especially in the document on poverty in the church. A few weeks before the bishops' meeting Gutiérrez outlined a "theology of liberation" in a talk in the coastal fishing port of Chimbote, Peru. That occasion may mark the first use of the expression in Latin America. In subsequent papers and talks Gutiérrez developed his ideas. During 1970 there was an explosion of conferences on the topic. In 1971 Gutiérrez and Hugo Assmann, a Brazilian, published full-length books on liberation theology that mapped the terrain of the emerging questions. While Gutiérrez' framework was primarily that of the Scriptures and modern theology, Assmann emphasized that what was developing was a new method of theology. In a similar vein the Argentine Enrique Dussel suggested a new way of reading Latin American church history and proposed philosophical categories appropriate to a situation of oppression.

Traditional Catholic theology had served to train priests in the seminary. It was in effect a defense of traditional Catholic doctrine against the onslaughts of Protestantism, the Enlightenment, and modernity in general. During the twentieth century Catholic theology slowly moved toward the university and began to adopt the critical methods of modern scholarship. Protestant theology was already more at home in the university.

Even in the early 1960s both Protestants and Catholics had intuitions of what would become a specific Latin American theology. Nevertheless, only late in the decade did they make a conscious break from the European matrix. It was the pressure of events, and especially the move from social to expressly political involvement mentioned above, that raised new questions. Theologians began to consciously take Latin America as their context for raising questions. As they realized that their theology was emerging out of a particular context, they began to see that the same thing was true of any theology—including the theology they had learned in Europe. What they had once taken to be simply theology—seemingly "universal"—they now began to see as a "North Atlantic" theology, a theology of the rich world. This was true not only of traditional theology but of the work of progressive Vatican II theologians like Karl Rahner, Edward Schillebeeckx, and Hans Küng. A Uruguayan layman, Alberto Methol Ferre, articulated this new consciousness in a polemic essay entitled "Church and Opulent Society" (1969).

Latin American theologians found that they were not only dealing with different issues but that their method, the very way they engaged in theology, was different. Since the Enlightenment the major challenge for Christianity in the West has been its credibility: how can modern people believe in ancient stories about the seas parting before Moses' wand, or about Jesus multiplying loaves and fishes or rising from the dead? Theologians have responded first by using historical and textual scholarship to sort out various layers of meaning, literary forms, myths and legends, in the Scripture, and then by finding points of contact or correlation in modern culture, points at which people can actually hear a message of salvation.

While Latin Americans can understand such questions, their basic concerns are different. Their question is not so much whether one can believe what Christianity affirms, but rather what relevance Christianity has in the struggle for a more just world. Gutiérrez defines theology as "critical reflection on praxis in the light of the word of God." It is a critique of how social structures treat the poor and how Christians and the church itself operate.

Yet liberation theology is not primarily an ethics. It is not a systematic exposition of principles on how people should act; rather it is an exploration of the theological meaning of such activity. Thus, for instance, Gutiérrez and other theologians accept the dependency critique advanced by social scientists. However, they go on to point out the biblical and theological resonances of the term "liberation." God is encountered in the people's struggle for liberation. Similarly, their concern is not to lay down specific rules for how to struggle for justice. They stress that a responsible commitment within class conflict is an expression of love for neighbor. They are not "fomenting" hatred, as critics contend; class conflict already exists. Through solidarity in struggle with the poor, class division must be transcended in a new type of society.

Early essays in liberation theology paid special attention to the church. In contrast to a strong anti-authority and anti-institution spirit that characterized the later 1960s elsewhere, Latin American Catholic theologians did not question the Roman Catholic church's fundamental hierarchical structure, although they pointed to the need for conversion. Some asked, for example, whether the Eucharist celebrated in a wealthy congregation might seem to endorse extravagant consumption that reduced others to inhuman poverty. In raising such questions theologians were not arguing that masses should be canceled but that the church should examine its presence in society and be prepared to make changes.

The initial sketches of liberation theology anticipated most of the major issues that would develop later. Church workers and active lay people now had a rationale for new options.

Christians for Socialism

Like Brazil earlier and Central America later, Chile was at the center of the Latin American stage in the late 1960s and early 1970s. The Popular Unity leftist coalition won national elections and under President Salvador Allende sought to carry out significant reforms. Other Latin Americans paid close attention. If socialism could come gradually and peacefully to Chile, it could be a sign of hope for others.

Chilean politics were atypical for Latin America. Democratic institutions seemed firmly established, labor unions were strong, and political parties embodied clear-cut competing ideologies. Many became disillusioned with the Christian Democrats' "Revolution in Liberty," especially after harsh repression of strikers in 1967. Critics claimed that Christian Democracy was not a "third way" between capitalism and communism, but simply reformist capitalism, incapable of solving Chile's problems. Significant groups of Christians joined left-wing parties and movements. The Allende coalition victory in 1970 signaled a growing leftward shift.

The advent of a socialist government raised new questions for Christians. The Christians for Socialism movement advocated direct political involvement. Its members believed Christians should accept the basic "rationality" of socialism, although they did not endorse any particular political group. Some were former Christian Democrats who had become radicalized and formed groups like MAPU (United Popular Action Movement) or the Christian Left; many joined MIR (Movement of the Revolutionary Left), which advocated going beyond electoral processes; some joined the Socialist Party; very few, however, became Communists. These Christians called for a new kind of pastoral presence within the move toward socialism. They insisted that since much of the worldview and ideology that had been preached and taught as Christianity hindered people from accepting socialism, Christians had a particular responsibility to free people of such ideological blockages.

In April 1982 some four hundred people converged in Santiago for an international conference of Christians for Socialism (despite the opposition of the Chilean bishops). Assmann, Gutiérrez, and a number of the liberation theologians were present. The conference's final document inevitably reflected the Chilean situation, for example, in its frequent denunciation of *tercerismo* ("third-wayism," i.e., Christian Democracy). The terminology is clearly Marxist, with frequent references to "relations of production, capitalist appropriation of surplus value, class struggle, ideological struggle," and so forth.

The conference called on Christians to engage in ideological struggle by identifying and "unmasking" the manipulation of Christianity to justify capitalism. However, this does not mean "instrumentalizing the faith for other political ends, but rather restoring to it its original evangelical dimension." (This question continues to recur: how is Christian involvement with the left different from the time-honored support the church has provided the conservative status quo?)

The document stated that Christians were discovering "the convergence between the radical nature of their faith and their political commitment." There was a "fertile interaction" between faith and revolutionary practice. Revolutionary practice was said to be "the generating matrix of a new theological creativity." Theology thus became "critical reflection within and about liberating praxis as part of a permanent confrontation with the demands of the Gospel."

The document closed with a line from Che Guevara that had been displayed on banners and signs during the meeting itself: "When Christians dare to give full-fledged revolutionary witness, then the Latin American revolution will be invincible. . . ."

2. GOING TO THE POOR

JOELMIR BETING, A BRAZILIAN JOURNALIST, CALLS HIS COUNTRY a "Belindia"—a Belgium plus an India. Thirty-two million people enjoy a standard of living like that of Belgium, a working class of around thirty million just gets by, and the remaining seventy million live in conditions of hunger, disease, and unemployment like those in India. He says they are "political prisoners of the system."

This fact of widespread poverty is the starting point for liberation theology.

In mid-1985 I was with a Witness for Peace delegation in an area of Nicaragua where peasants had been resettled away from a battle zone. The government had erected twenty-by-twenty-foot house frames, and each family had finished the walls and put up partitions. Most of the people in the community had not only never been to Managua, but had not been as far as the nearest paved road, about fifty miles away. Another member of the delegation and I were talking quietly with our hosts while one of the young men in the family kept a small fire going with wood chips. Running my eye around the walls in the flickering firelight, I suddenly realized that the total cash value of their possessions—a couple of pots, a few plastic dishes, utensils, a flashlight—was only a few dollars. What would it be like to live at that level of poverty? I couldn't really imagine it.

We were spending a couple of weeks in Nicaragua as a gesture of concern and solidarity. Yet I came away with a sense that despite my years of living with the poor in a Panamanian barrio and working with the poor in Guatemala, my own experience as an American separated me from them by a vast gulf.

Starting in the 1960s, many of the church pastoral workers—priests and sisters—made significant efforts to come closer to the poor. In so doing they faced new questions and issues. Liberation theology is the outgrowth of their efforts. Understanding that process requires a continual effort of moral imagination to keep present the reality of the poor.

My procedure here will be to parallel that movement. First, I will look at how poverty itself became an issue, and then at what was involved in the new approach to the poor (this chapter). Then I will look at the key elements of liberation theology's message for the poor and the new model of the church emerging in "basic Christian communities" (Chapters Three and Four). Only after seeing how liberation theology works at the village or barrio level will I turn to the structural, ideological, and institutional questions.

▪ ▪ ▪

Poverty as a Theological Issue

Although poverty was not a major theme in the documents of Vatican II, the self-criticism unleashed by the council began to raise questions about world poverty and about the church's attitude toward wealth and poverty. This kind of questioning soon became a central concern in Latin America.

The common stereotype that the Catholic church in Latin America has been on the side of the rich should not be accepted without qualification. In most countries, decades of anticlerical governments in the nineteenth century left the church institutionally weakened. Priests and sisters lived modestly. On the other hand, some religious orders and dioceses owned lands. Like doctors and other professionals, priests and sisters were concentrated in the cities, very often teaching in Catholic schools that served the upper and middle classes, who could afford tuition. The traditional rationalization was that these schools were providing future elites with a moral and religious foundation. Priests in rural areas saw most of their parishioners only on occasional ritual visits.

There was another angle to the growing awareness of the church's responsibility for the situation of poverty. Priests had indeed often preached resignation to "God's will" in a way that could reinforce the belief that the present distribution of wealth and power comes from God. Nevertheless, the role of priests and the institutional church should not be exaggerated. Most poor people had only occasional contact with representatives of the church. Peasant society itself tended to internalize a fixed and even fatalistic view of the universe with religious symbols and rationalizations, which was transmitted primarily by parents and grandparents and indeed the whole village culture. Priests only reinforced that view whenever they intoned, "Blessed are the poor in spirit."

Yet that saying comes from Jesus. How should poverty be

understood? Members of religious orders who were committed to the vow of poverty and who did not own property individually nevertheless enjoyed a standard of living and security that insulated them from the daily agony and anguish of the poor. Jesus' words, moreover, were meant for all his disciples.

The issue came down to two questions: what does the ideal of poverty mean in a situation where most people are suffering dehumanizing poverty, and what should the church and Christians do about poverty?

Gustavo Gutiérrez took an approach that was both biblical and responsive to the situation of the Latin American church. It had become so customary to speak of being "poor *in spirit*" that the wealthy, who imagined themselves to be "detached" from their possessions, could feel they were practicing poverty. Gutiérrez stressed that the Bible understands poverty—material poverty—as an evil, as the result of the oppression of some people by others. Poverty that dehumanizes human beings is an offense against God. To know God is to work to overcome poverty, to work for God's kingdom.

Yet there is another strain in the Bible, especially noteworthy in the Psalms, which sees in the poor the "faithful remnant" of Israel. "Understood in this way," says Gutiérrez, "poverty is opposed to pride, to an attitude of self-sufficiency; on the other hand, it is synonymous with faith, with abandonment and trust in the Lord."

Gutiérrez finds yet a third biblical approach to poverty in the Apostle Paul's image of Christ saving humankind: "He was rich, yet for your sake he became poor, so that through his poverty you might become rich" (2 Cor. 8:9). The church is called to a similar kind of solidarity.

Poverty thus has three interrelated meanings: dehumanizing lack of material goods, openness to God, commitment in solidarity. The Medellín document on the poverty of the church, which shows Gutiérrez' hand, proposes an ideal to strive for when it says that a poor church "denounces the unjust lack of goods of this world and the sin that causes it; preaches and lives spiritual poverty, as an attitude of spiritual childhood and openness to the Lord; and commits itself to material poverty."

Gutiérrez sees voluntary poverty as "an act of love and liberation" that has "redemptive value." Its deepest motivation is love of neighbor, and it is meaningful

> only as a commitment of solidarity with the poor, with those who suffer misery and injustice. The commitment is to witness to the evil which has resulted from sin and is a breach of communion. It is not a question of idealizing poverty, but rather of taking it on as it is—an evil—to protest against it and to struggle to abolish it.

Some have accused liberation theologians of identifying the poor with the proletariat in the Marxist sense. Perhaps these critics see the frequent reference to the "poor" as a kind of code language. In a Marxist understanding, however, "proletariat" is a technical term designating the class of those who must sell their labor power to the capitalist class. Strictly speaking, the proletariat, the industrial working class, and by extension the permanent plantation labor force, is a relatively small segment of Latin American society. Most of the poor are either peasants (and hence small property owners) or they are part of the informal economy in the city. Marx called these latter the "lumpenproletariat."

If Marxism were their primary frame of reference, Latin American theologians and those doing pastoral work would be very concerned to identify the genuine proletariat, the potentially revolutionary class, in order to work with them. In both their pastoral activity and theology, however, they are centered on those who are poor for no other reason than that they are poor. They believe that is what following Jesus today demands.

▪ ▪ ▪

Dialogue and *Concientización*

Supposing church people wished to take up poverty in commitment to the poor, what should they do?

A first step was simply to come into closer contact with them and find ways of sharing in their life. Hundreds, even thousands, of sisters and priests began to "go to the poor." Often this meant leaving a relatively comfortable life and going to a barrio or to a rural area to live in an adobe house or wooden shack like the people's. They would share at least some of the conditions of the people. In the countryside that might mean constantly having to walk hours through forest or jungle, while in a barrio it might mean standing in line in the early morning to get buckets of water, enduring dust and dirt during the dry season and mud during the rainy season, traveling on packed rickety buses that might take an hour or more to reach downtown. In some cases they would support themselves with a job in an office or school, or more rarely, in a factory. To the people of the barrios or towns it was initially a novelty to deal familiarly with priests and sisters whom they had always seen only in formal and ritualized contexts.

Although they might share many of the conditions of the poor, such people did not become poor themselves. They retained their education and culture, the security that is built into being a priest or sister, and their connections outside the barrio or town. They were in the village or barrio voluntarily and could always leave.

Going to the poor, however crucial, was only the first step. What else should they do? By the mid-1960s some church people had already acquired considerable experience in development projects, particularly cooperatives. But there was a growing awareness of the inadequacy of such efforts. Cooperatives do little for peasants who have little land, and they do nothing for the landless. *Desarrollismo*—"developmentalism"—

was the commonly heard pejorative term for Band-Aid reforms that failed to address the issues of power.

But what kind of a role should priests, sisters, and lay activists take? The model for engagement with the poor appeared in *concientización* (or in the Portuguese form *conscientização*). The term, which is roughly equivalent to "consciousness-raising," gained currency as a result of the work of the Brazilian educator Paulo Freire in the late 1950s and early 1960s. One element in the grass-roots organizing at that time was teaching peasants to read and write. Freire and others questioned the assumptions of traditional literacy training, which in giving adults the Brazilian equivalent of "Dick and Jane" reading materials was treating them like children. Instead, Freire and his associates assumed that the peasants they were working with were in fact adults, and intelligent adults—they merely lacked the linguistic tools needed for reading and writing. Hence, they used words and images from the adult world of the peasants: their crops, tools, customs, and so forth, referring even to issues of conflict and power like land tenure.

A typical session might begin with a poster or slide projection, showing, for instance, peasants harvesting a crop. To open the discussion the leader would simply ask, "What do we see here?" and encourage people to make observations. From the elements of the picture itself the discussion would move to their own work, its value, and the problem of making ends meet. The leader would strive to have people react to the picture rather than to himself or herself; the picture was a "codification" of their life situation, which they were "decoding" through dialogue. The leader's facilitation style was a reversal of the normal domineering or paternalistic patterns of leadership.

Only after some forty-five minutes or more of such discussion would the session move to reading skills. Freire and his associates had detected and chosen a number of "generative words," words denoting elemental realities in people's lives (e.g., "mother," "father," "land," "corn," "hoe") that also had elementary linguistic materials (*papa* uses only two letters). Even with their first few letters and syllables peasants would soon be building their own words rather than simply receiving them for drill (for example, changing one letter produces *pipa*, "pipe").

This sketchy treatment gives some idea of what was novel in the early *concientización* efforts. The constant stress on the peasants' experience and expression reversed the traditional top-down model of teaching in which one who "knows," the teacher, imparts knowledge to one who is presumed ignorant. Freire asserted that conventional pedagogical methods assumed a "banking idea" of education—they treated people as empty recipients into which knowledge could be deposited. Freire and his associates, by contrast, assumed that even poor people are "subjects." Using a Socratic technique that moved from effects (their own poverty) to causes (the power arrangements in society), they brought poor people to a critical consciousness. They also affirmed the culture of the peasants rather than seeking to introduce them into an alien culture.

One indication of the power of *conscientização* was the fact that peasants often learned to read in a few weeks. Organizers striving to form peasant leagues in northeastern Brazil used the method, and indeed it seemed to augur a whole new way whereby the poor could become actively involved in their own development. The experiment was cut short by the military coup of 1964, and Freire himself had to leave Brazil. For the rest of the decade his ideas and methods rapidly spread as people attended his lectures in Chile, where he worked with the agrarian reform agency, or in places like the language and culture training center run by Ivan Illich in Cuernavaca, Mexico.

The "Freire method" has provided a model of work in which outsiders—that is, people who are not themselves poor—can go to the popular classes in a nonpaternalistic way. As a method, it has given church people, social workers, and organizers a sense of what to do, whether directly in literacy classes, or in using the *concientización* approach to help the community come together, articulate its needs, and become organized. They can be what Antonio Gramsci calls "organic intellectuals."

Underlying this pedagogy of *concientización* is a humanistic philosophy. In Freire's books *Education for Critical Consciousness* and *Pedagogy of the Oppressed,* one finds a philosophical idiom that reflects Western philosophy from the Greeks to existentialism and Marxism. At first glance, such baggage might seem excessive for the tasks of teaching peasants to read. Yet it underscores something very radical in Freire. He believes that what philosophers have been saying about "man" for twenty-five hundred years is valid for Latin American poor people: that they are rational and political animals and have the capacity to enjoy or exercise freedom. This is precisely what the dominant society denies in practice if not in words.

Implicit in the "Freire method" is a political agenda that can be called revolutionary, although Freire and his followers are highly critical of all attempts to organize in a top-down manner. Those who go out to the barrios and countryside to do *concientización* often mistrust existing leftist political organizations, particularly the orthodox Communist parties. They believe that through a *concientización* process "the people" themselves must decide what sort of organizational approach they will take. Freire himself has worked with socialist and revolutionary governments in Tanzania, Guinea-Bissau, and Angola.

As church people became aware of the method and spirit of *concientización,* they came to see it as fitting very neatly into the emerging sense of how the church should opt for the poor. In several passages the Medellín documents use the term *concientización* and related ideas; the document on education is especially Freirean in spirit. This is all the more surprising in view of the fact that in 1968 church personnel were still overwhelmingly involved in private schools. Yet the bishops take a much wider view, focusing on those who are marginalized, calling for a "liberating education," and stating that education should be "democratized." Education should not mean incorporating people into existing cultural structures but "giving them the means so that they can be the agents of their own progress."

The bishops seem to be making proposals for society at large. But what about the church's education of its own members in the Christian faith? At Medellín the bishops in effect recognized that although Latin Americans have been Roman Catholic for four centuries, to some extent they have not heard the message of Christ, at least in its fullness. Hence, they spoke of an "evangelization of the baptized," or a "reevangelization of adults."

In short, as a result of the new awareness of poverty, church pastoral agents have sought to carry out the church's mission by sharing the lot of the poor and engaging them in a process of evangelization that would develop a critical consciousness.

Dialogues at Palo Seco

Just as Freire and his associates had worked their ideas into a practical method for teaching peasants to read, church people gradually worked out methods and courses to use at the local level. To form an idea of this pastoral approach let us imagine a village of some seventy-five houses which we will call Palo Seco. It sits in the hills some twenty kilometers by dirt road from the nearest town, San Jeronimo. For some time the pastor and sisters from the parish have been visiting the village and familiarizing themselves with its inhabitants. Now a group of people has agreed to attend a series of meetings.

The people are sitting on rough benches on the dirt floor of a small community center, most of them barefoot or in sandals, scrawny, somewhat shy. The woman who is to lead the discussion is an outsider. The only sign she is a nun is the wooden cross she is wearing. For a while Sister Elena makes small talk with the people. Then she prefaces the meeting by emphasizing that the idea is not for her to act like a teacher but rather for all of them to talk to each other as equals, since everyone has something worthwhile to contribute from his or her own experience.

She begins the session with an open-ended question, "Is there evil and injustice in the world?" People nod or say yes, but then there is silence, so she encourages them to bring up examples and they tell stories of political graft or other forms of injustice. With probing questions she gets them to examine some of these examples, and the discussion ranges over what injustice means. After forty-five minutes or so she says she would like to show an example of injustice from the Bible and slowly reads the narrative of Cain and Abel. The conclusion is that injustice is rooted in what the Bible calls "sin"—that is, when human beings refuse to care for their brothers and sisters and even go so far as to kill them.

In the next session the opening question is simply "What is God like?" Again there is an initial silence. With some encouragement people begin to draw out notions passed on through traditional catechism and the culture itself, such as the image of God as "Supreme Being," someone who is "always watching," a "Judge," or perhaps the image of "Father." After some discussion of the implications of some of these ideas, Sister Elena again brings out the Bible, this time to read from the third chapter of Exodus where God appears to Moses and says:

> I have witnessed the affliction of my people in Egypt and have heard their cry of complaint . . . so I know well what they are suffering. Therefore I have come down to rescue them from the hands of the Egyptians and lead them out of that land into a good and spacious land. [3:7–8]

She outlines the exodus narrative and they discuss what it means to say God hears the cry of his oppressed people and whether it is still valid today.

At another session there is a discussion of what brings fulfillment in human life. People tell stories about those who have sought money, or pleasure, or power, and examine the results. This time Sister Elena brings up the example of Jesus Christ, whose life was one of self-giving. True human fulfillment is found not in isolation but in service to others, especially in community.

Another discussion deals with relations between men and women, examining men's attitudes and the prevailing double standard about marital fidelity: what is completely unacceptable in a woman is accepted as common practice in men. This time they see that in the Bible the man-woman relationship, which some see as something sordid, is an image of the union between Christ and the church. Both men and women are called to be faithful to one another as Christ and the church are.

These examples may serve to give an idea of the general approach of an initial course. Such dialogues are an exploration of basic human experiences within the culture of the people themselves. The starting point might be a question, or a story that serves as a case study. The people reflect on it, add their own experiences and their own ideas, often in the form of proverbs or common folk wisdom. These are tested particularly through probing questions by the leader.

To some extent the biblical element is a reaffirmation of basic human experiences or popular culture (e.g., indignation at injustice), but it also challenges prevailing notions (e.g., cultural ideas of a distant, vengeful God, or macho double standards).

In such groups the poor not only feel their own worth affirmed, but they begin to question the assumption that society must be as it presently is—that such is "God's will"—and they began to question whether it might be otherwise. They may discuss how their own work as farmers is a fulfillment of the Genesis passages where the Lord puts the first human over all the birds and fish and animals and seed-bearing plants. They also note how human labor transforms the earth. From that point they may go on to see social systems as human, not divine, creations, and thus subject to further human action, including pressure from organized poor people. They begin to take what Freire calls a "transformative" stance toward the world.

Like Freirean consciousness-raising, this kind of pastoral work provokes opposition. In 1980 a moderate priest in the chancery office in San Salvador told me, "What we did was help the peasants come to an awareness of their own dignity and worth, and that's what the powerful can't forgive."

Church pastoral workers see this process as one of *evangelization*. For some readers that term might conjure up tent revivals and people rising to "declare for Jesus." However, evangelization means communicating the gospel, which itself means "good news." The good news is that God hears the cry of the poor and is with them in their suffering and struggle. Christian faith is not primarily a matter of believing in those personages and events recorded in the pages of the Scriptures but rather of finding the meaning of life now in terms of those basic scriptural symbols. The point is not simply that someone named Jesus somehow reappeared after his death in a land called Palestine in the far distant past but rather that his resurrection leads to new life even now.

Finally, just as Freirean *concientización* is not regarded as a process by which a teacher who knows imparts knowledge to an "ignorant" learner but rather as one by which both seek to understand the world together, in this kind of evangelization it often turns out that the representatives of the church, despite their superior knowledge of the Scriptures, find that they are being evangelized by the poor, whose insight into life and suffering, and into the biblical text, may be very deep.

What has been described here is simply the initial dialogue in the form of a course in an imaginary community. The process varies considerably. The starting point might be community problems such as the lack of safe drinking water or poor bus access. In some circumstances Bible passages might be read first and people would then relate them to their own experience. The essential element is a serious dialogue rooted in Christian faith that deals with real issues in people's lives, with at least some social dimension. Singing and spontaneous prayer are also part of the meeting.

Following the initial course, the participants might be invited to a weekend course for a deeper and more systematic presentation of this biblical vision. People from the community are gradually trained to lead the discussions themselves so that the presence of a priest or sister is no longer necessary. A *comunidad eclesial de base* (church base community) takes shape (further discussed in Chapter Four). Besides holding meetings and discussions the group sometimes takes common actions such as helping repair a house or leading a community effort to demand better service from the Ministry of Education. At some point or other the powerful may see the community as a threat and use intimidation or violence.

An Option for the Poor

Liberation theology is rooted in the pastoral shift going on in the Catholic church wherein significant numbers of church people have made an option to go to the poor and engage them in a reinterpretation of their own religious tradition in a way that is more biblically based and gives them a transformative rather than a fatalistic stance toward the world. The theologians themselves are involved in such work either directly or indirectly. It is out of that encounter with the poor that liberation theology's questions arise. Intellectually, liberation theology may incorporate elements of social science and Marxism, a reinterpretation of Latin American history, or contact with contemporary philosophy—e.g., hermeneutics—but the starting point to which it continually returns is this ongoing dialogue with the poor.

One point should be obvious from the very terminology. Only the nonpoor can "opt for" the poor. The notion of the option for the poor is a recognition that institutionally the Catholic church has been closer to the elites than to the poor. The point is not so much the material wealth of the church, which is in fact modest, but the use of the church's resources, the mindset of its personnel, and the overall way it conceives its mission.

The situation of Protestant churches is different. They are the result of a wave of missionary activity in the late nineteenth and early twentieth centuries. The established mainline churches, Methodist, Baptist, Presbyterian, Lutheran, Episcopalian, and so forth, took root among the middle and lower-middle classes. However, it is the fundamentalist or pentecostal-type churches that have spread most rapidly among the poor, partly because they require little formal instruction for their ministers, who are themselves poor. The more established churches, on the other hand, require at least some seminary training. Some Protestants in the mainline churches have questioned whether their message of individual salvation has reinforced the inequities in society.

As originally formulated by the bishops at Medellín, this option for the poor was a rediscovery and contemporary application of a central element in the Scriptures. As it was put into practice, this option became controversial and even conflictive. As will be noted in Chapter Six, it led to numerous church-state confrontations; the murder of dozens of priests and religious and thousands of active lay people; and numerous instances of arrest, beatings, torture, and intimidation.

It was not surprising that some church people were tempted to soften Medellín's original commitment. Emphasis on poverty could be made to appear as a Trojan horse for Marxism; hence, there was a renewed emphasis on poverty as a spiritual attitude. The very definition of poverty, as well as its consequences for the church, became polemical.

Meeting in Puebla, Mexico, in 1979, the Latin American bishops (CELAM) said: "We see the growing gap between rich and poor as a scandal and a contradiction to Christian existence. The luxury of a few becomes an insult to the wretched poverty of the vast masses. . . ." They spoke of this as a "situation of social sinfulness" and as a "grave structural conflict."

Speaking of poverty, the bishops reaffirmed Medellín's "clear and prophetic option expressing preference for, and solidarity with, the poor." They then stated, "We affirm the need for a conversion on the part of the whole Church to a preferential option for the poor, an option aimed at their integral liberation." The "preferential option for the poor" became a slogan encapsulating the central thrust of the Puebla meeting and endorsing solidarity with the poor as God's will for the church.

3. MIRROR OF LIFE

The Bible Read by the Poor

A GROUP OF AMERICANS IN 1985 IS MEETING WITH MEMBERS of basic Christian communities crowded into the parlor of the parish house in the town of La Trinidad in Nicaragua. An Old Testament scholar from Claremont, California, asks, "What are your favorite Bible passages?"

Different people speak up: "The Acts of the Apostles, where it describes how the early Christian communities shared their goods and no one was poor."

"The Exodus, where God hears the cry of his people and comes to liberate them."

"Where Jesus goes into the synagogue and says he has come 'to bring glad tidings to the poor, and to proclaim liberty to captives.' "

"Matthew 25, where Jesus says, 'Whatever you did for one of my least brothers or sisters you did it for me.' "

Had the question been asked elsewhere in Latin America people would have mentioned many of the same passages. To a degree liberation theology is already at work in the selection of the passages and the interpretative slant given them. The people did not discover these Bible passages spontaneously but as the result of interaction with priests, sisters, and lay church activists.

Here I will present some of the major scriptural motifs, with examples of how they are understood in the religious vision that is at the heart of liberation theology.

Creation

Familiar as the story of "Adam and Eve," the opening pages of the book of Genesis are the source of major themes. There are actually two creation accounts (Gen. 1:1–2:4a and 2:4b–25). The first is an account of the creation of the cosmos, which takes for granted the ancient Near Eastern conception of a flat earth with the sky as a dome overhead and waters beneath. Rather like a potter beginning with shapeless clay, the Lord begins with a "formless wasteland"; separates the primeval waters with a dome; and creates dry land, vegetation, the heavenly bodies, fish and birds, and so forth on successive "days." After each "day" comes a refrain, "God saw how good it was." Finally, on the sixth "day" cattle, creeping things, and wild animals of all kinds are created, and as a final crescendo God says:

> Let us make man in our image, after our likeness. Let them have dominion over the fish of the sea, the birds of the air, and the cattle, and over all the wild animals and all the creatures that crawl on the ground.

Latin American poor people, who have grown up around "seed-bearing plants" and have had the "beasts" in their backyard and even wandering through their dirt-floored houses, enjoy the Genesis stories. They are not troubled by cosmology; they understand that these are not scientific but poetic accounts written centuries ago in other lands, and that their message is about God's relationship to the world and human beings. "Creationism," the banner of some religious conservatives in the United States, is not an issue.

What is stressed is the goodness of creation. This runs counter to the traditional dualism of matter and spirit instilled by four centuries of Catholic catechism. Human beings are seen as the very image and likeness of God. The path to the knowledge of God goes through other human beings. That means not human beings in general, but the particular human beings in one's village or barrio.

God has placed human beings in charge of creation. Again, peasants know what it is to have "dominion" over animals and make the earth produce. Technology—their use of chemical fertilizers and pesticides, for example—is an extension of this dominion. This is an entry point for discussing the issue of "nature" and "culture" so stressed by Freire: even the poorest, most isolated peasants have and create culture and are involved in transforming the earth.

A reflection on the Genesis account can easily move into a discussion of whether God intends that a few individuals own most of the land while others have little or none. Indeed, the Spanish word *tierra* means "earth," "land," and "soil."

Genesis thus provides a powerful set of symbols for human dignity and human responsibility in the world.

In the second creation account God creates a man by breathing into clay. Since the man is alone and cannot find a "suitable partner" among the other creatures, the Lord puts him to sleep, takes a rib, and shapes a woman. The man exclaims:

> "This one, at last, is bone of my bones,
> and flesh of my flesh;
> this one shall be called 'woman,'
> for out of 'her man' this one has been taken."
> That is why a man leaves his father and mother and clings to his wife, and the two of them become one body. [2:23–24]

The folktale quality of this account can lead to a lively discussion among a group of Latin Americans. Certainly, from a feminist viewpoint the symbolism of woman being created from man's rib is but one example of the patriarchal mind-set that runs through the Scriptures. In Latin American pastoral pedagogy, however, the emphasis is on the equality of male and female. Even this text emphasizes the sacredness of the union of man and woman as "one body." That symbol can be a powerful challenge to the macho notion that it is natural for a man to "have" more than one woman.

In this reading of Genesis there is no concern for the story of the "fall," the banishment of Adam and Eve from Eden for eating the forbidden fruit. The prototype of sin is more likely to be Cain's murder of Abel. In any case, sin is treated not only as an individual transgression or failure but as a reality that affects social structures. Thus the bishops at Medellín spoke of a "situation of sin," and at Puebla they several times noted that sin has "personal and social dimensions." This reading is similar to what other contemporary theologians describe as the "sin of the world," which deeply penetrates human history and culture.

The dominant culture in Latin America tells the poor they don't count—that is its real message even if demagogically it may speak of their dignity and worth. Liberation theology's reading of Genesis accentuates those elements of the Bible that stress the goodness of creation, the dignity of the poor as God's very image, and their dominion over the earth and their rights to its fruits, as well as the beauty of committed love between man and woman.

Exodus—Prototype of Liberation

Without a doubt, the exodus is the central event in the Hebrew Scriptures, the event that constitutes Israel as a people. In the biblical narrative, Moses encounters the Lord in a burning bush and is commissioned to lead the people out of slavery. He first tries to convince the pharaoh of his power by bringing down a series of plagues (waters turning to blood; pestilence; locusts; and so forth). But the pharaoh remains obdurate until the last plague, the death of all the firstborn of both humans and animals, including the pharaoh's son. At that point he grants permission to leave and the Israelites depart through the Red Sea, which opens up before them. When the pharaoh changes his mind and pursues them, the waters return, drowning his troops. This act of deliverance is a basic paradigm of God's saving action.

In a Latin American reading the focus is on God's concern to liberate the people:

> I have witnessed the affliction of my people in Egypt and have heard their cry of complaint against their slave drivers so I know well what they are suffering. Therefore I have come down to rescue them from the hands of the Egyptians and lead them out of that land into a good and spacious land, a land flowing with milk and honey. . . . [Exod. 3:7–8]

This is a God who can hear the cry of the oppressed, who comes down, and who leads them to liberation. In 1973 a group of bishops in northeastern Brazil wrote a severe critique of the military dictatorship, then at the height of its power and self-assurance. They titled their pastoral letter "I Have Heard the Cry of My People" and framed their message with the exodus motif.

Such a reading pays relatively little attention to the miraculous elements, such as the plagues; rather, it focuses on the oppressive rule of the pharaoh and the dynamics of Moses' leadership, toward both the oppressor and the oppressed. The notion of liberating leaders is familiar from Latin American history—e.g., history books call Simón Bolívar, the most prominent independence leader, the "Liberator." From another angle the difficulty village or barrio leaders experience in bringing people to confront their own oppression gives them some understanding of Moses' exasperation with the infidelity and weakness of the Israelites.

"Exodus" is not simply an event but a pattern of deliverance that provides a key for interpreting the Scriptures and for interpreting present experience.

Prophets and Prophecy, Then and Now

Although its beginnings are to be found in the Mosaic religion itself, the classical age of Hebrew prophecy occurred during the eighth through the sixth centuries B.C., a time of great political, moral, and religious crisis. During the time in which they occupied the land of Canaan, the period recorded by the Book of Judges (1200–1050 B.C.), the Israelites existed as a federation of tribes. Subsequently, however, under military pressure from the Philistines, they became a monarchy under Saul. After a brief period of glory under David and Solomon, they divided into two kingdoms.

In both the northern and southern kingdoms and in captivity, the classical prophets denounced idolatry, the exploitation of the poor by the powerful, and the infidelity of rulers who did not trust the Lord. Their message was both political and religious—indeed, it is plain that the prophets made no such distinction.

Some of their oracles sound quite contemporary in Latin

America today. Thus, Amos speaks of "you who trample upon the needy and destroy the poor of the land!" He portrays them as gloating:

"We will . . . fix our scales for cheating!
We will buy the lowly man for silver,
and the poor man for a pair of sandals;
even the refuse of the wheat we will sell!" [8:5–6]

Micah pictures the exploiters scheming day and night:

They covet fields, and seize them;
houses, and they take them;
they cheat an owner of his house,
a man of his inheritance. [2:2]

To Guatemalans these words describe the way generals and landholders have seized land, often from the peasants who have cleared it.

In a common scriptural image, Isaiah pictures the Lord as in a great courtroom rising to accuse the people, and especially the leaders:

"It is you who have devoured the vineyard;
the loot wrested from the poor is in your house.
What do you mean by crushing my people,
and grinding down the poor when they look to you?" [3:14–15]

Another line of prophecy that resonates today is the critique of any religion that emphasizes cult at the expense of justice and mercy. Amos has the Lord speak this condemnation:

"I hate, I spurn your feasts,
I take no pleasure in your solemnities;
. . . . Away with your noisy songs!
I will not listen to the melodies of your harps.
But if you would offer me holocausts,

then let justice surge like water,
and goodness like an unfailing stream." [5:21–25]

In a similar vein Hosea has the Lord say, "For it is love that I desire, not sacrifice, and knowledge of God rather than holocausts" (6:6). Such a notion is indeed a revelation to those accustomed to seeing Catholicism embodied in ornate churches, incense-filled ceremonies, and solemn, brocaded ecclesiastics. Some have taken to heart this critique. In El Salvador, Archbishop Oscar Romero left the cathedral construction unfinished in order to use the church's scarce resources for the poor and for pastoral work.

Although much of their message is dire warning, the prophets also offer the vision of a "new heaven and a new earth," a day when people will not toil in vain and children will not be suddenly destroyed.

The biblical prophets are generally outsiders, not a part of the religious establishment of priests and official prophets. Most of them are poor. Amos, for example, is originally a shepherd, and Micah comes from an obscure village. They prophesy calamities to come, not through some future-reading technique, but by reading the "signs of the times." Using Freirean terminology, J. Severino Croatto, the Argentine biblical scholar, calls the prophets the "conscientizers" of the people.

Latin Americans see prophecy not only in biblical texts but continuing in the church today. In his short but densely packed book *Monseñor Romero, Verdadero Profeta* (Archbishop Romero, True Prophet), Jon Sobrino argues that Romero was a prophet in the strict theological sense. He gives many examples of the archbishop's denunciation of idolatry (of money, of military and political power), of U.S. imperialism, of corruption and falsehood, and shows that these denunciations are rooted in the word of God.

There is a general recognition that the church is itself called to act prophetically. At the Puebla meeting in 1979 the bishops spoke of the church being "sent out as a prophetic People to announce the Gospel or discern the Lord's calls in history," to "announce where the presence of the Lord's spirit is manifested," and to "denounce where the mystery of iniquity is at work through deeds and structures that prevent more fraternal participation in the construction of society and in the enjoyment of the goods that God created for all."

Jesus: Struggle, Death, Vindication

Christ's figure is a familiar part of the landscape in Latin America. Yet, for the most part, that Jesus is a silent presence, like the statue of the Christ of Corcovado standing with his arms stretched out over Rio de Janeiro. When people discuss the gospel accounts in small groups, their familiar stereotypes are challenged and they encounter a different kind of Jesus figure.

A key passage is Luke's account of Jesus visiting Nazareth, his hometown, at the outset of his public life. He enters the synagogue on the sabbath, and like a visiting rabbi he is handed a scroll and finds a passage originally from Isaiah:

> "The spirit of the Lord is upon me;
> therefore, he has anointed me.
> He has sent me to bring glad tidings to the poor,
> to proclaim liberty to captives,
> recovery of sight to the blind
> and release to prisoners,
> to announce a year of favor from the Lord." [4:18–19]

Latin Americans see this as a kind of manifesto. Jesus is saying that the age of liberation foretold by the prophets is present in him.

Jesus does not preach himself, however, but the kingdom of God. When he cures people, it is a sign of the kingdom, and when he multiplies a few loaves and fishes in order to feed several thousand people, it is a sign of the banquet that is to be celebrated when the Messiah comes. Latin Americans interpret this to mean that the church should not focus on itself, but on serving the kingdom, which is much broader than the church, since to some extent the kingdom is drawing near wherever human beings are achieving justice and love.

Jesus lives poor, associates with the poor, and preaches poverty. He praises God, his Father: "for what you have hidden from the learned and clever you have revealed to the merest children" (Matt. 11:25). He says: "Blessed are you poor, the reign of God is yours. . . . But woe to you rich, for your consolation is now" (Luke 6:20, 24). When a rich young man approaches and asks what he must do to be saved, Jesus summarizes the commandments. The young man says he has observed them all and asks what else he should do. Jesus tells him to sell his possessions, give the proceeds to the poor, and follow him. As the young man goes away in sorrow, Jesus drives home the point: "It is easier for a camel to pass through a needle's eye than for a rich man to enter the kingdom of God" (Matt. 19:16–24).

Centuries of emphasizing poverty "of spirit" have taken the edge off these texts. The Latin American reading seeks to emphasize that Jesus is talking about real material poverty and wealth.

An often cited passage is found in Matthew 25, where Jesus pictures the final judgment. The nations are assembled before the Son of Man, who separates them into two groups "as a shepherd separates sheep from goats." He invites one group to "inherit the kingdom":

> For I was hungry and you gave me food, I was thirsty and you gave me drink. I was a stranger and you welcomed me, naked and you clothed me. I was ill and you comforted me, in prison and you came to visit me.

They ask when they saw him hungry, thirsty, and so forth, and he replies, "I assure you, as often as you did it for one of my least brothers, you did it for me." He then turns to those on the other side and says, "I was hungry and you gave me no food," and so forth, finishing with the statement, "I assure you, as often as you neglected to do it to one of these least ones, you neglected to do it to me" (Matt. 25:31–46).

Here practical material aid for one's neighbor is the criterion of a just life. Furthermore, in the person of those who are poor and in need stands Jesus himself, although neither those who aid nor those who refuse to do so recognize him. The criterion is not whether one considers oneself Christian or not—one might even be an atheist—but whether one has served the needs of others.

From the beginning Jesus' message and actions provoke opposition. After the scene in the synagogue mentioned above, he says, "No prophet gains acceptance in his native place," and reminds his hearers that over the centuries Israel has also ignored and even killed the prophets. The people become angry, expel him from the town, and try to throw him off a cliff, but he walks straight through the crowd and leaves (Luke 4:23–30). This insistence on the constant conflict in Jesus' life is a corrective to the traditional emphasis on his "meekness."

Jesus makes enemies with his denunciation of ritualized religion without love of neighbor. He denounces as hypocrites those who carry out minute rules while neglecting the most important elements, "justice and mercy and good faith." Jesus' attitude toward religion applies not only to his own time but is rather the basis for a permanent critique: all the institutions of religion—churches or cathedrals; vestments, incense, or sacraments; laws, rules, or customs; religious orders, dioceses, or the Vatican—all are means, not ends. True sacredness—indeed, the divine presence—is to be found in the other people who are at hand, and particularly in the poor and outcast, those whom the "world"—the power structure—disregards.

The early Christian communities that collected and edited Jesus' sayings into the gospels themselves suffered persecution. Hence, it is not surprising that they cherished passages such as:

> "Blest are you when they insult you and persecute you and utter every kind of slander against you because of me.
> Be glad and rejoice, for your reward is great in heaven;
> they persecuted the prophets before you in the very same way."
> [Matt. 5:11–12]

This text has had a very contemporary sound in Central America, where armies have singled out catechists as prime targets for abduction, torture, and murder and where peasants have often had to store their Bibles in underground hiding places.

Traditionally, the death of Jesus has been represented as a "sacrifice" and as something fated, something he had to undergo to carry out God's will or plan. Indeed, in many places the gospels quote Old Testament verses as proof that Jesus' suffering and death had been foreseen by the prophets. The customary reading thus saw Jesus as a human/divine "victim" in a cosmic drama—all the characters seemed to be playing out a foreordained script.

Contemporary readings, and especially in Latin America, seek to recover the human dimension of Jesus. His life is seen as one of struggle and uncertainty, one in which people, including Jesus himself, make real human decisions, with all their consequences. Thus, Jesus' execution by the authorities of both "church" and "state" of his time is a direct consequence of his message, which is correctly seen as "subversive" of the existing order.

Jesus really dies and is buried. However, something unheard of, something unimaginable, occurs. He appears to some of his women disciples, and to the Twelve, as well as others. His tomb is discovered to be empty. Finally, he commissions his disciples to carry on his word: "And know that I am with you always, until the end of the world" (Matt. 28:20). The realization that he is alive and still with them comes to be the central conviction of his followers.

Whatever the "historical" core of the resurrection narratives, they signal God's vindication of Jesus' life and message. It is not in vain to live and struggle as Jesus did, and in fact it leads to fullness of life. To accept the resurrection turns the meaning of life and death inside out. Fullness of life comes by way of death. That is the sense of the sayings the gospels attribute to Jesus. "One who wishes to come after me must deny his or her very self, take up the cross, and begin to follow in my footsteps. Whoever would save his or her life will lose it, but whoever loses his or her life for my sake will find it" (Matt. 16:24–25).

Many Latin Americans have internalized this conviction about life and death—they are willing to die if they must. Archbishop Romero of San Salvador expressed the conviction of many committed Latin American Christians when he said, "If they kill me, I will rise in the Salvadoran people." Since he was indeed murdered (while saying mass) and lives in the hearts of many people, he provides a contemporary example of the paradigm of death/resurrection embodied in Jesus.

Life in the First Base Communities

In Latin America today the Bible is read in small village- or barrio-level groups by people sitting on benches, often in the dim light of a kerosene lamp. Previously accustomed to seeing the church as the priest, or the large church building down in the town, or an organization with its own authorities like those of the government, they now begin to see themselves as the church. Jesus said, "Where two or three are gathered in my name, there am I in their midst" (Matt. 18:20).

They learn that in fact the first several generations of Jesus' followers did not have special church buildings but met in their own homes. Speaking of the first Christian community in Jerusalem, the Acts of the Apostles states:

> The community of believers were of one heart and one mind. None of them ever claimed anything as his own; rather, everything was held in common. With power the apostles bore witness to the resurrection of the Lord Jesus, and great respect was paid to them all; nor was there anyone needy among them, for all who owned property or houses sold them and lay them at the feet of the apostles to be distributed to everyone according to his need. [Acts 4:32–35; see also 2:42–47]

(That this was probably an idealized portrait only underscores the fact that the biblical authors see such sharing and common life as normative.)

Latin Americans can read the New Testament as recording the life of the first *comunidades de base*. They are encouraged to discover that although their small communities are an innovation within traditional Latin American Catholicism, they are closer to the churches set up by the apostles than the large parishes where individuals remain anonymous. Their own experience of starting new communities, of the sense of enthusiasm at discovering the message of the gospels, and their own sense of mission enables them to identify with the story of Paul and his missionary efforts around the Mediterranean world.

The numerous ethical instructions in the New Testament, sometimes in the form of long series of maxims or catalogues of virtues, are always grounded in affirmations about the basis for a new type of life. Thus, Paul says: "It was for liberty that Christ freed us. So stand firm, and do not take on yourselves the yoke of slavery a second time!" He explains:

> My brothers, remember that you have been called to live in freedom—but not a freedom that gives free rein to the flesh. Out of love, place yourselves at one another's service. The whole law has found its fulfillment in this one saying: "You shall love your neighbor as yourself." [Gal. 5:1, 13–14]

Elsewhere he explains that Christians have died and risen in Christ, and draws the consequences.

> What you have done is put aside your old self with its past deeds and put on a new man, one who grows in knowledge as he is formed anew in the image of his Creator. There is no Greek or Jew here, circumcised or uncircumcised, foreigner, Scythian, slave or freeman. Rather, Christ is everything in all of you. [Col. 3:9–11]

The phrase "new man" has a particular resonance for some Latin Americans, since Che Guevara and other Marxists also speak of a revolutionary "new man" (a few are sensitized enough to add "and woman").

Many New Testament passages emphasize the mystical unity between Christ and his followers, which is the basis for unity among believers. All are "one body" in Christ. Paul stresses that the members of the Christian community have different charisms (gifts), which complement each other, as do the members of the body. All are to serve, including those whose charism is leadership. "None of us lives as his own master and none of us dies as his own master. Both in life and in death we are the Lord's" (Rom. 14:7–8).

The highest level of this mystique of love and unity is found in the First Letter of John:

> God is love,
> and he who abides in love
> abides in God,
> and God in him. [4:16]

The radicality of this vision is its direct affirmation both that God is love and that the only way to know what love is to love other human beings.

The New Testament communities are tiny minorities, statistically insignificant within the vast Roman Empire. They also experience many problems, including persecution. Nevertheless, just as the Hebrew prophets hold out a vision of hope for their hearers in even the darkest days of captivity and exile, the New Testament proposes a vision of a radically changed cosmos, especially in the vision of Revelation, the last book in the Bible. In the "new Jerusalem" when God dwells with the people, "He shall wipe every tear from their eyes, and there shall be no more death or mourning, crying out or pain, for the former world has passed away" (Rev. 21:1–4).

Experience-Text-Experience: the "Hermeneutic Circle"

In this survey of biblical motifs and how they are interpreted from a liberationist perspective, I have been using the present tense. People find their own experience reflected in the Bible. The Brazilian Frei Betto says that priests tend to see the Bible as a kind of window they peek out of with curiosity. The people in base communities, however, "look at the Bible as in a mirror to see their own reality."

They understand the Bible in terms of their experience and reinterpret that experience in terms of biblical symbols. In theological jargon this is called the "hermeneutical circle"—interpretation moves from experience to text to experience. As an example, consider the saying of Jesus, "Unless the grain of wheat falls to the earth and dies, it remains just a grain of wheat. But if it dies, it produces much fruit" (John 12:24). The original text certainly applies to Jesus' own death. Suppose, however, a community leader is murdered, and after initial fear and intimidation, people resolve to continue their struggle, inspired by the leader's example. When that same text comes up, it is seen to refer to their martyred leader, whose life is showing fruit. Hence, there is an ongoing interaction between life experience and its interpretation in the light of the Scripture.

In this kind of Scripture reading people find both validation—as in those passages that emphasize God's preferential love for the poor—and challenge—as in Jesus' command to love one's enemies.

Liberation theology is quite biblical, but it is not literalist or fundamentalist. Prior to the Enlightenment the churches simply assumed that the Scriptures were the result of a direct dictation by God to Moses, the evangelists, and other biblical authors. Only slowly and painfully have the churches accepted historical and critical methods that revealed, for example, that the supposed "Mosaic" books were the result of many centuries of tradition. Similarly, the gospels give access to Jesus only through the eyes of Christian communities several decades after his life. The "Sermon on the Mount," for example, is not a verbatim record of Jesus but a collection of sayings attributed to him. Only in the last twenty-five years has Catholicism fully accepted the results of modern biblical scholarship.

Latin American theologians today do not belabor these points but take advantage of available scholarships. For example, Jesus' miracles are viewed not primarily as proofs of a divine origin but as signs. Jesus' feeding of five thousand people with a few loaves and fishes is taken as a sign of the messianic banquet. Did Jesus indeed "multiply" loaves and fishes? A generation ago the emphasis was on the divine power manifest in such ability to "suspend" the laws of nature. Scholarship today shows that the authors themselves were most intent to see the occasion as a sign of the promised messianic banquet present already inchoatively in Jesus. Hence, to see this account as expressing Jesus' solidarity with the poor and as a sign of the kingdom is closer to the original sense than to take it as part of a rationalistically constructed chain of reasoning moving from Jesus' power and authority to his "founding" of a church, and the transmission of that authority to the present church through the pope and bishops.

The aim of this chapter is primarily to communicate the main lines of the interpretation of Christian faith that is at the heart of liberation theology. For readers who are themselves believing Christians there will be many points of contact with a familiar faith. I can imagine, however, that some may be left with a very basic question: do these theologians really believe all this? After all, they have studied in European universities, they can read several languages, they are familiar with the complexities of Marxism. Do they ever wonder—late at night, perhaps—whether this is not after all simply a kind of language game?

Although I cannot answer for the Latin American theologians, I think the question is worth at least a modest consideration. Certainly, in their own lifetimes most of these theologians have seen their own understanding of Christianity undergo change. Their belief may be less literal than it was twenty-five or thirty years ago. Nevertheless, I think their answer might be that their faith has been deepened and validated by their experience with poor people. There is a very traditional mystical current in theology, called "negative theology," that asserts that God is more unlike than like any human representation—including biblical images. Thus, at the heart of the universe is utter mystery, a mystery that eludes any human grasp. God—ultimate mystery—is ever greater than our imagination. Yet it is only through love and commitment that we enter into contact with this mystery.

The firmness of faith comes not from particular concepts—even those of liberation theology or the Bible itself—but from commitment to a certain kind of life, exemplified in Jesus Christ and lived today by many ordinary men and women in Latin America. In the commitment of their brothers and sisters, theologians find their own faith fortified and validated.

4. A NEW MODEL OF CHURCH

Christian Base Communities

THE REFORMATION WAS MORE THAN THE THEOLOGICAL IDEAS of Luther, Calvin, and others. It was a broad movement embodied in new kinds of church congregations, with a new kind of leadership—pastors instead of Catholic priests. Similarly, although they are not the creation of liberation theology, the base communities are a primary embodiment of liberation theology. In Brazil alone it is estimated that there are more than seventy thousand such communities with a total membership of two and a half million people. Cardinal Ratzinger, the head of the Vatican agency charged with supervising doctrine, has warned that the ideas of liberation theology are "widely popularized under a simplified form" in base communities, which accept them uncritically. For their part, armies and police are often suspicious of such communities and target them for repression.

Church base communities *(comunidades eclesiales de base)* may be defined as small lay-led communities, motivated by Christian faith, that see themselves as part of the church and that are committed to working together to improve their communities and to establish a more just society.

The Rise of Base Communities

Like liberation theology, base communities are a response to a set of problems experienced in pastoral work. As noted in Chapter One, parishes in rural areas and in the shantytowns surrounding the cities often left one priest with twenty thousand or more baptized Catholics. Religious practice was low: in most countries 5 percent or fewer of the people would attend Sunday mass. Men in particular kept their distance from the church. The "popular Catholicism" of the majority of the people had little to do with the official rites and doctrines of the church but seemed to be focused on prayers to saints. In Brazil, spiritist cults continued to expand, and everywhere Protestant churches, which did not need a celibate, seminary-trained clergy, were making advances.

How were the ideals of church renewal, laid out at the Second Vatican Council, to become a reality among the vast majority of Latin American Catholics? It would take far more than celebrating the mass in Spanish or Portuguese. What was required was a new model of the church.

I have dwelt on the challenge facing the Catholic church after Vatican II because I believe it is important to see the base communities as the result of a pastoral response to that challenge. They are not a spontaneous effort on the part of the poor, but the result of an initiative by the church's pastoral agents, mainly sisters and priests, among the poor. It is only at a further stage that the poor themselves become active agents in the process.

The base communities were not created *ex nihilo*. Several movements within the church and pastoral experimentation dating back to the 1950s provided antecedents. One of the most important such antecedents is what was called "specialized Catholic Action." Early in this century, when even the bishops and the pope recognized that the European working classes had been "lost" to the church, the Belgian priest Joseph Cardign began a new approach to young working people. Contacting young factory workers outside the parish structure, Cardign began holding small group meetings that stressed not doctrine but action around people's real problems, such as unjust treatment by a foreman, or union struggles, or a coworker's needs. The method was summed up in three words "observe-judge-act." Participants would observe by discussing the relevant facts, judge by deciding whether the situation was in accord with the gospel, and agree to act in some way, however small. At the next meeting they would evaluate whether they had in fact fulfilled their commitment and what impact it might have had. The priest did not lead the discussion; he trained the leaders and acted as chaplain and advisor.

Cardign's work developed into a movement called JOC (Jeunesse Ouvrière Chrétienne—Young Christian Workers). Parallel movements for university and high school students and the family (Christian Family Movement) also arose under Cardign's inspiration. All these movements came to Latin America during the 1950s.

With their small cell structure, their focus on experience rather than doctrine, and their concern for action, they were important antecedents to today's base communities. Nevertheless, they continued to reflect their European origins. Their priest chaplains were little concerned to spread these movements, often limiting themselves to two or three cells. In Europe these chaplains were inspired by a mystique of establishing a presence in the midst of a "de-Christianized" milieu. Latin

Americans, however, were not alienated from religion like working-class Europeans. The base communities would take a process similar to observe-judge-act but would replicate it on a wide scale in villages and barrios rather than in the particular "milieux" of workplace and school.

Important antecedents are also to be found in church renewal movements that developed primarily among professional and business groups. The Cursillos de Cristiandad, developed in Spain, were a kind of weekend retreat, carefully structured to lead to an emotional conversion experience. Having become *cursillistas,* people continued to gather for regular follow-up meetings, and promoted further *cursillos* among their friends and associates. Many became *cursillo* activists, by being trained to give conferences recounting their own conversion. *Cursillo* morality focused on sins of marital infidelity or drinking, or treatment of other individuals, and was little concerned about the impact of social structures. Most of the participants were from the wealthy or professional classes, and they set the tone; the poor who participated might initially feel attracted by the apparent air of Christian "brotherhood," but they soon came to question its depth and sincerity.

The exact starting point for base communities themselves cannot be determined with precision. What is clear is that pastoral experimentation in a number of places prepared the ground. Some point to what happened in one community called Barra do Piraí near Rio de Janeiro in 1957. A woman lamented that on Christmas Eve three Protestant chapels had been full of people, singing, while the Catholic church was "closed and dark! . . . Because we can't get a priest." She took the matter to Bishop Agnelo Rossi, who decided to train people to be catechists who could gather the people for a weekly, or even daily, prayer service, even what was called "priestless Mass." It is only by hindsight, however, that such an incident can be seen as leading to base communities. Indeed, catechists were trained in many Latin American countries. While such lay-led groups would have much in common with the subsequent base communities, they were under clerical control and seem to have been primarily devotional, with little interest in community issues. The First Nationwide Pastoral Plan (1965–70) of the Brazilian bishops was already calling for subdividing present parishes into "basic communities."

In 1963 a group of priests from Chicago, under the leadership of Leo Mahon, began an experimental kind of pastoral work on the outskirts of Panama City with adult dialogue groups. They developed most of the features of the kind of pedagogy described in Chapters Two and Three and had an enormous influence. From the mid-1970s onward, hundreds of priests, sisters, and lay people visited San Miguelito, and many adapted its methods throughout Latin America.

By the end of the 1960s the base-community model had gained wide acceptance, even though many clergy resisted. At Medellín the bishops stated that the church should become present in small local communities, forming a core community of faith, hope, and charity. They saw the base community as the "initial cell" for building the church and the "focal point for evangelization." They also saw that it could make an important contribution to development efforts. CELAM (Latin American Bishops' Conference) training institutes in Chile, Colombia, and Ecuador spread the ideas and methodology of "base communities." Two priests, José Marins, a Brazilian, and Edgard Beltrán, a Colombian, traveled full-time giving courses on them throughout Latin America.

Theologians and social theorists were providing a rationale for this new kind of pastoral work. They pointed out that the New Testament communities were "house-churches." Hence, the base communities were retrieving a forgotten tradition. Sociologists pointed out that, as opposed to larger parish structure where individuals were lost in an anonymous mass, the small community favored commitment, personal growth, dialogue, and critical thinking. Some suggested that the base community should become the basic cell of the church and that the parish should become essentially a network of such communities, wherein the priest or sister would be a trainer, facilitator, and spiritual guide.

To sum up, the "basic Christian communities" arose out of a critical awareness of the inadequacy of existing pastoral models, the results of some earlier pastoral efforts based on small groups, initial experiments in a number of countries, and a rationale supplied by theologians and sociologists.

It has been the poor who have responded to base-community pastoral work. The very word "base" is usually understood to mean the "bottom" of society, that is, the poor majority. Such communities have been organized either in rural areas or in the shantytowns surrounding large cities. It is the poor who feel the need to come together. Moreover, church workers find it easiest to establish base communities in rural areas. In urban shantytowns people have more distractions, such as TV, and lead a more harried life (for example, distances and crowded public transport mean that workers often arrive home late and have to rise very early) and may be initially suspicious of outsiders and even of their neighbors.

In general, base communities have not taken root in middle- and upper-class Catholicism. Such people continue to be served by Catholic schools, and parishes not unlike Catholic parishes in the United States and Europe, as well as by movements (the Cursillo de Cristiandad, the Christian Family Movement).

Base communities can arise in different manners. Many have started with a dialogue course such as the one described in Chapter Two. Others have started with "Bible circles"—that is, the biblical text itself serves as the starting point for discussion. In other cases a priest or sister may be involved with a community, helping it organize to struggle for its rights, and then gradually lead the community, or some members of it, to reflect and pray over the significance of their community involvement. In practice, the religious and social activities of a community tend to mesh. A group may meet to read the Bible, sing, reflect, and pray—and then go on to discuss the situation of a cooperative, or go out to fix a road so buses and trucks can get to the village.

▪ ▪ ▪

Popular Religion

Traditional Latin American Catholicism's most characteristic expressions are found in popular religiosity, such as processions and devotion to saints. In Holy Week there might be great pageants representing Jesus' last days. Individuals who are sick or unemployed might promise the Virgin Mary that if the problems are solved they will make a pilgrimage or undergo a particular penance. To foreigners and local elites such practices are evidence of peasant superstition. The identity of Protestants has been bound up with their own rejection of this religiosity. For the majority, however, it has been a source of consolation and strength for centuries.

Prior to the Second Vatican Council popular Catholicism was not in itself a pastoral problem. Priest and people might participate in the same rite with very different interpretations. For example, in performing a baptism the priest might believe he was taking away original sin, while the people might conceive of baptism as a medicine against illness or as conveying a kind of citizenship. The people's religiosity was part and parcel of a larger worldview quite removed from the priest's. Neither side really engaged the other.

With Vatican II and the general modernizing movement that accompanied it, popular religion became something of a problem. It seemed at odds with the Catholic renewal in every respect: it seemed to stress outward observance rather than inner conviction; it seemed to be based on legends about the saints rather than on the gospel of Jesus Christ; its concern seemed to be religious practices rather than the ethical demands of love.

Secularization, a buzzword during the immediate postcouncil period, suggested a straight-line evolution away from religiosity. If so, popular religiosity was destined to disappear. Some theologians and pastoral theorists, influenced, at least indirectly, by

Karl Barth, were willing to welcome secularization since in their view Christianity was not a religion. (Those unfamiliar with modern theology might find that assertion strange. In the Barthian view natural human religiosity and the many religions in history all represent human efforts to reach God and in fact are forms of idolatry. What the Bible presents has nothing in common with religion: it is God's revelation to human beings, which is contrary to all human expectation.)

Whatever their theology or theories of secularization, many priests felt uneasy toward popular religiosity. Some went so far as to remove saints' statues from churches. They tried to teach a more biblical, interiorized form of Christian faith. It became common to require parents to attend instructions before they could have their children baptized.

In general, the church and its personnel were out of touch with popular religion. In 1969 the Vatican itself, in order to streamline the church calendar, announced that some saints' days were being eliminated. More surprisingly, Vatican authorities acknowledged that there was no historical proof that some saints had even existed, including the widely popular Saint Christopher, patron saint of travelers. Those Latin Americans who heard of the decision were incensed. A fisherman told me it was as if they had lined up the people's favorite saints in front of a firing squad.

Before long, however, pastoral workers and theologians took a second, more critical look at their approach to popular Catholicism. They noted that there was no need to accept European analyses of secularization and the accompanying theologies. They sought to comprehend popular religion in the context of popular culture as a whole. That culture was an understandable response to a situation of poverty and domination. If, for example, people are systematically prevented from having any real power, it is not surprising that they seek powerful advocates in heaven. If many people without access to modern medicine see their children die, it is not surprising that they should see baptism as a possible remedy. In fact, since colonial times religion has enabled people to hold up and resist under very difficult conditions and to make sense out of life. Popular religion, instead of being judged as "massifying," could be seen as expressing a suppressed aspiration to peoplehood.

Methodologically, respect for the people's religiosity came to mean listening before teaching, seeking to understand and then to help people themselves come to a critical awareness of their own religious traditions and practices. This might be seen as applying the *concientización* philosophy to the religious realm as well as to society. In some cases the people might decide to change their traditional practices. For example, a community might make a conscious collective decision to control or eliminate alcohol at a patron saint's feast, not out of narrowly moralistic reasons, but because they were being exploited by the liquor manufacturers and because when they got drunk they were disfiguring the image of God within them. In other cases they might put a new, more biblical, interpretation on an existing practice. Thus, a procession might be seen as a symbol of the ancient Exodus from Egypt and the march toward liberation today.

Social Impact

Base communities, as I have been emphasizing, have arisen as a pastoral response on the part of the Catholic church. The initial motivation of the priests and sisters who started them was to fulfill their own mission by finding a more appropriate form of the church for poor Latin Americans. Their aim was not political. To this day many base communities are essentially pastoral and not political—at least not in any conflictive way.

What has attracted attention, however, has been the political potential of these groups, especially in the most extreme circumstances, as in Central America, where base-community pastoral work prepared the soil for grass-roots organization and revolutionary struggle.

To counter what might be an exaggerated idea of such communities, it is well to keep in mind that only a small proportion of the population participates in base communities. In any given country only a minority of parishes—perhaps 10 percent—have adopted this model of pastoral work. In some rural dioceses, where pastoral teams cooperate across parish lines, the percentage might be considerably higher, while in some capital cities with millions of inhabitants, very few parishes, even in the outlying shantytowns, have serious base-community-style work. Secondly, even where base communities are highly developed, only a minority of people become active, ongoing participants. In Aguilares, El Salvador, for example, starting in 1972, a well-organized group of Jesuits began this type of work. After considerable systematic work they had established ten communities in the towns and twenty-seven in the outlying villages. In their evaluation, they estimated that of the 30,000 inhabitants of the area, no more than 5,000 had some sense of the gospel, for 2,000 it meant something, and about 400 could be said to be committed. Somewhat later they estimated that an average of 673 people attended the weekly "celebration of the Word" in the base communities. Despite the considerable attention given to base communities in Nicaragua, far less than 1 percent of the population participates in them. Even in Brazil, where these communities are most developed, somewhat under 2 percent of the country participates actively in base communities.

To put it another way, there are several times as many active Protestants and evangelicals as there are members of Catholic base communities. Such quantitative considerations are important for maintaining a sense of proportion. The importance of base communities is primarily qualitative.

The social and political impact of base communities may be viewed in terms of (1) initial consciousness-raising, (2) their vision of life and motivation for involvement, (3) the sense of community and mutual aid and support they generate, (4) the experience of grass-roots democracy, (5) the direct actions they engage in, and (6) directly political effects.

The initial stages of *concientización*, what the people themselves often call their "awakening," have been described in Chapter Two. Perhaps the most essential element goes beyond the particular subject matter, and is the very act of questioning the way things are. Base communities use a methodology based on questions. In addition, the people also acquire some simple categories of analysis. At a weekend course, after they have pooled their own perceptions of an issue such as land tenure, a discussion leader may provide them with some statistics that enable them to appreciate where their experience fits into the larger context of their country as a whole. Or there may be a whole session on class differences, with the people providing their descriptions of the various classes. Using their own perceptions, the discussion leader might then take a marker pen and draw their society in the form of a pyramid. Critics might denounce this as instilling class antagonism; others might counter that it simply means helping people systematize what they have already observed and experienced.

As described in Chapter Three, the Scriptures provide a series of symbols that outline an ideal of life. People acquire a strong sense that as human beings they are called to be active agents in history. Various biblical texts provide images of what human life should be—a society of brothers and sisters, a life of sharing and equality. If intended for society at large this is certainly a utopian vision. For grass-roots Christians this utopia provides a distant ideal or goal, which could never be realized in its entirety. Yet poor Latin Americans find that ideal more understandable and energizing than what Marxism offers in such phrases as "a classless society."

Part of what makes such notions powerful is that people have seen their effect, albeit in very modest ways, at the local level. Experience together in the base community may have lowered previously existing barriers of suspicion. In some cases village or family feuds have been settled. Common work projects for the community are another source of unity.

Traditionally, local community leaders have tended to copy the existing models of the dominant society, by themselves being petty dictators or at most demagogic populists. By sharing leadership widely and seeking to act by consensus, base communities have given many people a sense of a grass-roots kind of democratic process. That experience in turn has made them more critical of existing political procedures.

Sometimes the people of the base community themselves decide to initiate an action or to become involved in an action. A Brazilian writes, for example, of cases where people surrounded and captured a plantation owner who was treating them unjustly, took him by force to army authorities, and secured his commitment not to continue. Base communities have also been involved in land invasions. Such actions are nonviolent and, indeed, the existing organized networks of active nonviolence in Latin America, coordinated by Adolfo Pérez Esquivel, the Argentine Nobel Prize winner, are mainly networks of base communities.

Base communities have undeniable spin-off effects in the political process. They function in effect as cadre schools, primarily for leadership within the church. Leadership qualities developed there, however, may have spin-offs elsewhere. In Central America the mass organizations of peasants developed out of soil prepared by church pastoral work. Often at the village level the same people who had formed the base community would become members of a militant peasant organization. In their own minds there was a direct continuity between their awakening through the gospel, their own local organizing efforts, and their decision to join a national peasant organization. One Nicaraguan organizer later said the Sandinistas regarded the base communities as "quarries" for their own organizing.

During the worst years of dictatorship in Brazil, the base communities provided a small space in which people could reaffirm their dignity and hope. As the military gradually eased the most severe repression and the country prepared to move back to representative democratic forms, there was considerable uneasiness among the base communities and the pastoral agents working with them. Pastoral agents were wary of the political process. Some were no doubt resentful that politicians might simply scoop off leaders whom they had spent years developing. In a more principled way some church people argued that any meaningful change had to come from the grass roots and hence they rejected political parties. This attitude received the pejorative label *basismo*—"grass-rootsism."

Some Brazilians thought the base communities would channel their members toward one particular political option, especially voting for the Workers Party. Pastoral teams did have courses and educational materials aimed at developing a critical consciousness about the political process. Base communities discussed the criteria for making a political choice. Surveys showed that they voted overwhelmingly for opposition parties, but they did not provide a bloc vote for any particular party.

Base Communities and the Wider Church

As they have grown in numbers, base communities have raised a number of questions: Are they a new model of the church, destined to spread until they are the norm? What do they imply for the Catholic church institution as a whole?

Obviously, lay-led groups of poor people might not mesh neatly with the vertical authority system of the Catholic church. Church authorities like to see base communities as simply a convenient subdivision of the parish; consequently, each community is under the authority of the pastor, who is in turn under the bishop. The base community is simply the lowest subdivision of the worldwide Roman Catholic church. In practice, such a conception would keep base communities under the permanent tutelage of the clergy.

However, base communities have shown a growing ability to assume responsibility and take initiatives. A series of national congresses held in Brazil exemplifies this trend. Attending the first meeting, held in Vitória, Espírito Santo, in 1975, were a half-dozen bishops, some experts, more than twenty pastoral workers, and a few members of such communities. Some one hundred people attended the second such meeting, also in Vitória, half of them from base communities. This time grass-roots groups had sent in about a hundred reports, which the theologians, social scientists, and so forth studied, and from which they drew up conclusions that were passed back to the groups. Two-thirds of the two hundred people who attended the third meeting, held in João Pessoa, in northeastern Brazil, in 1978, were from the grass roots, and they took charge of organizing the whole meeting. According to Leonardo Boff, the participants were virtually unanimous on two points: (1) the main root of the oppression they suffer is the elitist, exclusive, capitalist system; and (2) people resist and are liberated to the extent that they become united and create a network of popular movements. At the Fourth Congress in Itaici, in the state of São Paulo in 1981, there were three hundred people representing seventy-one dioceses, while the fifth, held in Canindé, Ceara, in the drought-stricken Northeast, was even more in the hands of the lay people themselves.

What is notable is not lay participation as such but the fact that poor people have taken a strong leadership role in the base-community movement at the national level in Brazil. Initially, they had to learn procedures like running meetings, taking notes, and coming to consensus from the middle-class pastoral workers, but they are making the movement increasingly their own.

There are indications that people from base communities may be assuming another kind of responsibility. Normally, base communities have developed only where priests or sisters have worked to set them up. The leaders are then chosen from the local community. In recent years, however, there are instances of lay people themselves taking on a "missionary" role. That is, they feel a call to leave their own community and travel to other communities, rather like the image of itinerant apostolic missionaries presented in the New Testament. This kind of initiative seems to stretch the limits of normal church structures.

In the long run, these developments threaten the way the Catholic church has operated. At Medellín (1968) the bishops had recommended the formation of base communities unreservedly. During the later 1970s they had been put on their guard. Critics objected to the term "popular church" or "people's church," emphasizing that the church is born of the Holy Spirit and not out of any particular social class. The phrase "popular church" was in fact a shortened form of a slogan used at the 1975 meeting in Brazil: "A Church Born of the People Through the Spirit of God."

Base communities, along with the notion of a "people's church," were thus controversial when the Latin American bishops met in Puebla in 1979. Along with words of praise for base communities, the bishops had words of caution and warning. They insisted that the church must be viewed "as a historically, socially structured People" that "represents the broader, more universal, and better defined structure in which the life of the base communities must be inscribed if they are not to fall prey to the danger of organizational anarchy or narrow-minded, sectarian elitism." Curiously, the bishops, the church's top management, who enjoy the privileges of the major elites in Latin American societies, were suggesting that poor Christians in barrios or villages run the risk of being elites. Theologically, they were asserting that the base communities are incomplete without the institutions of the broader church—that is, the parish and the diocese.

Rather than attack base communities head-on, however, Puebla's approach is to envelop them in an overall ecclesiology where they are subordinated to the hierarchical institution. The argument is worth following for what it reveals of the uses of theology.

In their most direct description of how base communities work, the bishops stress religious aspects, although they mention commitment to justice, solidarity, and commitment. The term "base" is taken in the sense of a cell in an organism rather than that of being on the bottom of a class society. In this passage there is no mention of liberation but rather of building a "civilization of love" (Paul VI's phrase, frequently cited in the Puebla documents). Base communities are said to "embody the Church's preferential love for the common people."

The bishops present the church as more fully present in the parish and even more fully present in the diocese. The Eucharist is celebrated in the parish, which "overcomes the limitations inherent in small communities." The diocese enjoys a "primacy" among church communities because it is presided over by a bishop. Such a bishop-centered view is not surprising in a document prepared by bishops, and there is support for it in the documents of Vatican II.

The question of where the church is "present" can be posed in another way, however. One could say that the church is present where it is most directly engaged in its evangelizing mission, most in touch with the suffering and struggle of the people, and bearing a word of hope. From that perspective the church would be most "present" in small communities on the front lines. The institutional elements of the church, including the bishops and the pope, would exist to serve the spread of the kingdom. The church should exhibit a radical egalitarianism in which neither bishop nor pope is superior to a lay leader in the remote reaches of the Amazon. The difference is one of function. From participants' descriptions it would seem that the later congresses of base communities in Brazil have modestly begun to prefigure that situation. For example, the clerics and even bishops are indistinguishable from the rest (except by wearing glasses or having a paunch) and all must wait their turn to speak.

The argument that the celebration of the Eucharist in the parish makes the church more fully present there can be turned around. If the "front lines" of the church are with the base community, it would seem fitting that the people should be able to celebrate the Lord's Supper regularly. If a "priest shortage" makes that impossible, the Catholic system for preparing and ordaining priests should be questioned and reexamined. In itself, celebrating the Eucharist does not require years in the seminary; in fact, it requires little more training than what the lay leaders already have. Why not, then, change the church's discipline and allow people from the community—women as well as men—to be designated and ordained?

Obviously, such a practice would run up against the Vatican's repeated refusal to consider either married priests or women priests. Since the base communities regard themselves as part of the Catholic church and have no desire to split away, they can discreetly raise the issue but not resolve it themselves.

While some critics have attempted to portray base communities as anti-institutional or as potentially schismatic, those involved in the movement are clear that they do not reject the institutional framework of the Roman Catholic church. They accept it not only for pragmatic or tactical reasons but out of theological conviction. In this sense Latin American liberation theologians are more conservative than many in Europe or the United States.

It is the nonpoor who make an "option for the poor." To what extent the Roman Catholic church as a whole will not only opt *for* the poor but become a church *of* the poor remains an open question.

5. FEET-ON-THE-GROUND

From Experience to Theology

FOR SEVERAL YEARS CLODOVIS BOFF, A THEOLOGIAN LIKE HIS more famous brother Leonardo, spent half the year teaching in Rio de Janeiro and the other half doing pastoral work with priests and sisters in the state of Acre at the western end of the Amazon basin near Bolivia. He collected his notes from 1983 into a kind of "theological journal," published with the title *Teologia Pê-no-Chão* (Feet-on-the-Ground Theology). His reflections range from pastoral questions about the meaning of sacraments like baptism or the Eucharist among the people, to the exploitation of the rubber gatherers of the region and the gradual disappearance of their way of life, to his own misery as he walks long hours through the jungle with an infected foot, to his delight at coming across thousands of butterflies in a clearing.

A few years previously he had published *Teologia e Prática*, the most thorough treatment of theological methodology by a Latin American. In that work he made extensive use of the ideas of theoreticians like Bachelard, Bourdieu, Gadamer, Habermas, Ricoeur, Piaget, and Foucault, as well as the major modern theologians.

In going to Acre, Boff was no doubt consciously opting to bring himself down to earth—actually to jungle mud. And yet in what he did he was not repudiating his theoretical work, much less taking up an anti-intellectual stand.

Liberation theologians are intellectuals. They produce a steady output of books and articles and take part in conferences. What makes their enterprise different from most academic theology, and from the usual role of the intellectual, however, is its connection to grass-roots work and popular movements.

They have an impact on events, and their own work is affected by their involvement with popular forces. Their aim is to be "organic intellectuals" (Antonio Gramsci)—that is, intellectuals whose work is directly connected with popular struggle.

The preceding three chapters have focused largely on pastoral work at the village or barrio level. Of course, some kind of theology is already at work there, at least implicitly, for example, in the choice of biblical passages emphasized and in the interpretive key used. Later chapters will deal with particular institutional and ideological questions that have arisen out of such pastoral work. At this point I would like to make some observations on the nexus between liberation theology and experience by looking at the intended audience, the relationship between theory and practice, the use of social theory, and the theological sense of "liberation."

Two false extremes can help focus the question. Those who see liberation theology as a threat typically view the theologian and pastoral workers as infecting the church with Marxism under the guise of theology. At the opposite extreme some perhaps romantically see theologians as distilling the wisdom already present in the base communities. Theologians would be rapporteurs of what is happening on the grass roots.

That formulation suggests that I regard neither description as accurate. As a preliminary generalization I will state that liberation is both prior to pastoral work and the outgrowth of pastoral work. It is both theory-*for*-praxis and theory-*of*-praxis.

Audience

In sharply divided societies like those in Latin America, there is little meaningful contact across class lines. Obviously, the poor do not have access to the upper elites. It is almost equally true, moreover, that the village or barrio is a closed world to outsiders. Even barrio or village officials and merchants are culturally similar to their neighbors.

In this respect church personnel are an exception. Consider, for example, a sister in a shantytown. She can actually choose to live in the area, sharing the day-to-day life. She may be university-educated, and through her order and other connections she is part of a much wider network. Her ability to become part of the local community is considerably greater than that of other outside "intellectuals" such as social workers or university-connected organizers. After she has lived there for a period, the people will consider her part of the community. She brings her organizational skills and her ability to articulate issues.

More than any other outsiders, church personnel—sisters, priests, pastors—are able to cross cultural and class lines. This of course is what makes them a danger in the eyes of landholders or colonels.

Most liberation theologians live like these pastoral workers, often in shantytowns or other poor neighborhoods. They spend some of their time doing pastoral work themselves and give frequent workshops or short courses for priests, sisters, and lay people doing pastoral work. Only a fraction of their time is spent on conventional classroom teaching. When they write, their primary audience, I believe, is made up of those doing pastoral work.

For the most part, they do not write directly for the poor. Few ordinary poor people, even if they could read, would get much out of Gustavo Gutiérrez' works, for example. Some theologians have also written simple devotional books. Carlos Mesters, a Dutchman who has spent years in Brazil, has written numerous pamphlets explaining the Bible in simple, comprehensible language, using references to Brazilian popular culture.

Other clergy, and bishops in particular, are a further audience. Much of what the theologians write is in effect a defense of the liberating model of pastoral work. Thus, theologians liberally quote official church documents or show how what is done today is in fact in line with the most authentic church tradition. A further audience is made up of theological colleagues in Europe, North America, and the rest of the Third World.

Jon Sobrino's essay "Unity and Conflict in the Church" may illustrate these points. During the late 1970s the rise of the "popular organizations" in El Salvador was not only a threat to the existing military-dominated government but a source of tension in the Catholic church. To a great extent these organizations had arisen out of soil prepared by pastoral work. They became increasingly militant and expressed their critique of society in Marxist language. For landholders and the military, priests were the "brains" who had incited the peasants. Things reached such a pass that in mid-1978 four of the bishops stated that Christians could not belong to these organizations, while Archbishop Romero and Bishop Rivera y Damas defended them (see Chapter Eight).

It was this experience of division that pushed Sobrino to the typewriter, even though he does not mention El Salvador by name. His overall aim is to find the theological basis for the unity of the church. Sobrino moves beyond the conventional Catholic approach, which would see in the hierarchy the solution to all questions of unity. A major principle is that the church exists not for itself but to serve the kingdom of God. In situations of conflict the church must find its unity around service to the poor. Moreover, some tension between prophecy and institution should be expected. To phrase the point more sharply than Sobrino might, those who "divide" the church through their commitment to justice might be serving genuine church unity more than those who simply hide behind hierarchical positions. Sobrino does not solve the problem—again, he does not even mention the country that prompted his reflection—but he provides a theological basis for dealing with the painful experience of conflict within the church.

To return to the question of audience, it is clear that such an essay would be most useful to those on the "front lines" of the church, priests and sisters accused of fomenting division. Their accusers might be bishops and might even use terms from the Bible or from Vatican II. Sobrino's essay would help them deal with such accusations.

People in villages and barrios, on the other hand, might be little concerned about "church unity," since the whole ecclesiastical milieu would be quite far removed from their experience. They would be affected only if, for example, the bishop decided to discipline or transfer their pastor.

Critics of liberation theology may not be convinced by Sobrino's arguments, but at least it confronts them with a critique of their own position that is grounded in Scripture and theological scholarship.

Finally, Sobrino's theological peers in other parts of the world might find his argument helpful if they faced similar kinds of division. On the other hand, if they normally look at the question of church unity in strictly theological or biblical terms, or from the viewpoint of the ecumenical movement. Sobrino's formulation might suggest a different perspective.

Liberation theology's primary interlocutors, then, are those doing pastoral work (and only through them the poor themselves); other groups in the church, including the hierarchy; and other theologians. Its questions and methods derive largely from this set of interlocutors.

Experience and Theory

A discussion of theory and practice reveals clear cultural differences between the intellectual milieux of North America (and often Western Europe as well) and Latin America. In our everyday usage "theory" is often contrasted pejoratively with "reality." We tend to take as normative the "scientific method" in which theory is the result of an empirical, self-correcting trial-and-error process.

Among Latin American intellectuals, on the other hand, "empirical" is most often a pejorative term, denoting superficial appearance rather than the deep reality of things. Theory is regarded as a tool for cutting through appearance to get at the heart of things. Many essays by Latin American social scientists, for example, seem to be focused largely on constructing a "theoretical framework." Concrete data often seem to take second place. What Latin Americans understand as "praxis" is poles apart from Yankee "practicality."

Gustavo Gutiérrez insists that, as reflection, theology is "second act": the first act is commitment to the poor. In a first and most basic sense the procedure is not from doctrine to application or from the general to the particular. In the instance just cited, Sobrino's starting point was a problem being experienced in the life of the church. Only after laying out the problem did he search for theological criteria for dealing with it. A more conventional approach would have been a top-down insistence that there could be no problem of conflict in the church as long as one obeyed the bishop.

The notion of the "primacy of praxis" is sometimes presented in contrast to the customary stress on orthodoxy in traditional Catholic theology. Using a play on words, many theologians insist that ortho-praxis (right acting) is ultimately more important than ortho-doxy (right doctrine). The aim of theology, then, should be to aid Christians to do what God wants and not merely to adhere to correct doctrinal formulas. A Christology, for example, will point to the contemporary implications of the way Jesus lived, rather than concentrate on the various heresies that led the church to elaborate dogmatic clarifications. Still, it would be superficial to conclude that Latin American theologians are not concerned about orthodoxy.

Often the term "praxis" refers to its usage in the works of Paulo Freire, namely, as action with reflection. Action without reflection can be misguided. At its worst, reflection without action is armchair revolution. Peasants forming an organization or catechists coming together can spend hours or days in discussion. Nevertheless, such time spent together eventually leads to a very tenacious commitment. "Reflective action" is very real at the level of grass-roots pastoral work.

At the beginning of this chapter I suggested that liberation theology is both theory-*for*-praxis (it has its own input to grass-roots action in the form of criteria, methods, and so forth) and theory-*of*-praxis (it is "second act" and its questions and insights come from involvement with the grass roots).

While most Latin American theologians tend to emphasize this "listening" aspect, Juan Luis Segundo has written of "Two Theologies of Liberation." He points out that the initial formulations were the work of theologians involved not so much with the poor as with university groups and intellectuals who were becoming aware of the structural crisis of Latin America. Coming to an "ideological suspicion" that existing forms of Christianity were strongly affected by dominant ideologies, they conceived of their work as one of unmasking "the anti-Christian elements hidden in a so-called Christian society."

He sees a second line of liberation theology as having arisen subsequently in connection with pastoral work among poor people. Pastoral agents and theologians felt that they should learn from the poor. One sign of this shift was a more positive assessment of popular religiosity. He believes, however, that there is some contradiction here. He points out that theologians who profess to be learning from the people are also eager to reorient their religiosity, for example, by shifting their focus away from Jesus' cross alone to a fuller, more liberating sense of salvation that includes the resurrection.

I believe Segundo is right to correct a too naive idea that the theologians are simply learning from the people. They have their own contribution to make from their scholarly knowledge of the Bible and church history, and perhaps a more systematic view of how society works.

Theology and Social Theory

I have described liberation theology in terms of three closely related tasks: to reinterpret Christian faith in terms of the bleak lot of the poor; to criticize society and its ideologies through theology; and to observe and comment on the practices of the church itself, and of Christians. Such a theology makes, necessarily, a conscious use of social science or social theory. That is something new in Catholic theology. Latin Americans see social theory as providing analytical tools, somewhat as philosophy provided tools for classical theology.

There are many social theories, however. How should one be chosen over another? Clodovis Boff notes that the question is twofold: which kind of theory *explains more* (scientific criteria) and which kind of theory will be *more effective* for achieving the ends or realizing the values one regards as most important (ethical criteria).

Clodovis' brother Leonardo distinguishes two broad kinds of social theory: "the functionalist, which sees society by and large as an organic whole; and the dialectical, which sees it in a special way as a complexus of forces in tension and conflict by reason of the divergency of their interests." The term "functionalist" here may echo Talcott Parsons, but it is applied to all views in which it is assumed that society is normally in equilibrium and any conflicts are resolved within the existing social system. "Dialectical" social science assumes that conflicts may lead to a systemic change.

For that very reason Boff states that liberation theology opts for a dialectical kind of analysis—that is, one that analyzes "conflicts and imbalances affecting the impoverished and calls for a reformulation of the social system itself . . . in order to secure . . . justice for all its members." Such analysis "better answers to the objectives of faith and Christian practice."

In other words, Latin American theologians opt for what would be called a radical social science in the United States. Like many Latin American social scientists they see mainstream social science as more descriptive than explanatory. Their primary concern is to understand the social structures they live under in order to change those structures. They are not interested in fine-tuning the workings of existing society.

Latin American social science came into its own with its critique of existing models of development and of theories of development—called by the general term "dependence theory." Early theories of development emphasized themes such as growth, modernization, nationalism, democratic institutions, planning, infrastructure, and institution building. Even in the 1950s economists working in the United Nations Economic Commission for Latin America began questioning the assumption that "backward" nations could achieve development by following the path already traced out by the "advanced" nations. They pointed to a history of domination and colonialism by those countries that were first to industrialize—Great Britain, followed by the United States and other European countries. These countries of the "center" had set up an international division of labor in which the role of the "periphery" (the Third World) was to produce agricultural products and minerals. These economies were misshapen by exaggerated concentration on export and could not develop autonomously in accordance with their own needs. Prices for these export products fluctuated wildly. Moreover, over the long run the terms of trade seemed to continually deteriorate. Thus, for example, an imported truck would cost more and more bags of coffee.

Economically speaking, the countries of the periphery have existed for the center. Bolivian Indians died in the mines because of the Spanish Crown's desire for gold. During the height of the Brazilian rubber boom, landholders in Manaus in the heart of the Amazon basin could even build an opera house and contract entire Italian opera companies to come a thousand miles upriver. When rubber trees could be grown cheaper in Malaya, the boom abruptly stopped and the opera house was abandoned. Similarly, Latin American industrialization since World War II has served the needs of multinational corporations seeking cheap labor and ways to produce consumer goods for the elite, not necessarily to serve the needs of the poor majorities of Latin America.

Third World countries cannot develop autonomously in accordance with their own needs; they are dependent on decisions taken elsewhere. Their elites are dependent elites; they are essentially local allies and intermediaries for the dominant countries of the center.

Dependence is obvious in politics and culture as well. The center lays down the parameters of what is tolerable and reacts when the boundaries are crossed (U.S. actions against the Allende government in Chile, for example). Cultural dependence is manifest in the way the elites and middle classes mimic fashions, fads, and ideas from the rich countries.

"Dependence theory" refers not to a single theory but to a whole body of theory. Dependence is a new paradigm, a new way of posing the problem of development. Raúl Prebisch, one of the U.N. economists who proposed the center-periphery formulation, gave this definition of dependence late in his career:

> By dependence I mean the relations between centres and the periphery whereby a country is subjected to decisions taken in the centres, not only in economic matters, but also in patterns of politics and strategy for domestic and foreign policies. The consequence is that due to exterior pressure the country cannot decide autonomously what it should do or cease doing.

Prebisch and others believed that dependency was not inherent in capitalism. A truly national bourgeoisie, aided by the right kind of policies, such as protection for nascent industries, could be the agents of a genuinely autonomous development. The fact that from the 1930s to the 1950s, when Europe and the United States were occupied with the Great Depression and World War II, both Argentina and Brazil began their own independent, inward-directed industrialization seemed to illustrate this possibility. That is, Latin American countries could free themselves from the domination of the "center" and engage in their own independent capitalist development. Dependency theory could provide the basis for a reformist government program. In and of itself, dependence theory is not necessarily Marxist.

Many writers, however, went on to critique capitalism as such. They believed that capitalism has been shaping Latin America for centuries. Even during the colonial period, it was nascent European mercantile capitalism that drained off Latin American mineral wealth. Latin American economies may have had feudal traits, but they were integrated into a world economic system that was already capitalist. These more radical critics see the national bourgeoisie as so linked to international capital that they are incapable of breaking free and seeking autonomous development. Reformism is insufficient; the kind of changes needed can come about only through revolution.

"Dependency theory" has gone far beyond Latin America, and indeed there are many formulations of what can be called a structural critique of the present world economic order. One school is that of "world-systems theory" associated with Immanuel Wallerstein. For their part Marxist theorists have reacted against approaches centered on trade relations and have focused attention on modes of production. While not denying the initial insight of dependency theory—that underdevelopment is structural—they have sought to understand it in a more detailed way by concentrating on the way labor and the means of production have been organized.

Whatever their differences, these approaches agree in their critique of present models of development and the theories that sustain them. The very notion of "development" is misleading insofar as it sees change as essentially an unfolding—a gradual, incremental process. When the Latin American economies are effectively controlled by oligarchical-military elites and the world economy is dominated by the wealthy Western countries, "development" cannot lead to a decent life for the poor majority.

"Liberation" entails a break with the present order in which Latin American countries could establish sufficient autonomy to reshape their economies to serve the needs of that poor majority. The term "liberation" is understood in contradistinction to "development."

Although they would agree that such a systemic change entails some form of socialism, liberation theologians do not spell out what they mean in detail. In only one of his three books does Gutiérrez even take up the notion of socialism explicitly, and that only in a few short passages. In a 1974 essay, "Capitalism vs. Socialism: Crux Theologica," Juan Luis Segundo states:

> By "socialism" I do not mean a complete, long-term social project—hence one that is endowed with a particular ideology or philosophy. I simply mean a political regime in which the ownership of the means of production is taken away from individuals and handed over to higher institutions whose main concern is the common good. By "capitalism" I mean a political regime in which the ownership of the goods of production is left open to economic competition.
>
> Some might ask here: Why not spell out the socialist model more fully: Or why not talk about the possibility of a moderated, renovated capitalism? For a very simple reason, I would reply. We are not seers, nor are we capable of controlling the world of the future. The only real and possible option open to us lies within our own countries. Right now today the only thing we can do is to decide whether or not we are going to give individuals or private groups the right to own the means of

> production that exist in our countries. And that decision is what I call the option between capitalism and socialism.

Note that Segundo does not invoke the longer-range myths of Marxism, such as the advent of a classless society. (Segundo's central concern in this essay is not to define his idea of socialism but to discuss on what grounds Christians can commit themselves politically.)

Segundo and other liberation theologians clearly do not feel the obligation to spell out in detail what kind of society they envision. Perhaps they believe that it is not their proper function as theologians to provide a blueprint. I think they see such a socialism as having three characteristics: (1) people's basic needs will be met, (2) ordinary people will themselves be active agents in building a new society, and (3) what is created will not be a copy of existing socialisms but a genuinely Latin American creation. In a socialist society exploitation will be ended. None will live in luxury by monopolizing lands and other productive factories, while others, including the workers whose labor produces the wealth, live in misery. The economy will be restructured so that the first priorities are job creation and the production of basic food and consumer items. Export production will serve to generate new investment and not luxury consumption.

A catchphrase from the Medellín documents is that people should be "subjects of their own development." A socialist society should be a participatory society. The institutions of such participation should begin at the village level. Such participation should be far more democratic than the present institutions of formal democracy, which in Latin America serve to mask the real powerlessness of ordinary people.

Latin Americans emphasize that the socialism they have in mind must be proper to each country and cannot be copied from other models. They are convinced that each revolution can learn from the accumulated experience of the past, including the mistakes, and need not follow the same script. Normally, they do not write lengthy critiques of "actually existing socialism" (the USSR and Eastern Europe), although they often refer to it with shorthand expressions like "bureaucratized socialism."

In my opinion the experience of the Sandinista revolution since 1979 has injected greater realism into the discussion of what "liberation" might mean for Latin American countries. Nicaragua has remained within the Western economic system, and internally it retains a market economy, 60 percent of which is in private hands. Michael Conroy, an economist at the University of Texas, states that the Nicaraguan government has followed the economic strategy urged by writers of the "structuralist" school of Latin American economists, such as Prebisch, rather than the prescriptions of radical Marxists. Through its "hegemony" the Sandinista government seeks to impose what it calls the "logic of the majority" on an economy that continues to operate primarily through market mechanisms.

"Integral" Liberation

For the most part, Latin American theologians have not contributed to social theory but have simply accepted the quasi-consensus of Latin American social theorists that basic structural change—liberation—is necessary. It is their own task as theologians to develop the theological and pastoral implications of this position.

As a way into this question, imagine again the community of Palo Seco discussing the meaning of the biblical phrase "kingdom of God." They agree that it is God's will that people live together in harmony and solidarity, helping one another. That is what they are modestly attempting in their own community, and they are aware of similar efforts elsewhere. They believe that they are experiencing God's kingdom in their midst. At the same time, they realize that present structures put people at odds with one another. If God's kingdom is to be realized in society at large, they must become linked to others on a broader scale.

This position raises fundamental questions. Isn't the proper role of the church "religious"? What is the connection between their own efforts and God's kingdom? Isn't it dangerous to confuse the human and the divine, or the material and the spiritual?

Traditional Catholicism presented human life as a transitory phase on the way to "heaven"; earthly life was essentially a kind of trial. Vatican II reversed that by stressing the continuity between "temporal progress" and ultimate "transcendence."

Pope Paul VI provided an emphatic example of this continuity in his encyclical *Populorum Progressio.* Critiquing narrowly technocratic approaches to development, he advocated rather "integral development," which he defined as "the transition from less human conditions to those which are more human." He catalogued these conditions in a kind of ascending order of human development. From the less human conditions of poverty and exploitation, through humanizing conditions, including not only overcoming poverty but growing in knowledge and culture, cooperation with others, and a will to peace, all the way to acknowledgment of God and being joined to God in faith and love, the pope saw continuity—seemingly an unbroken continuum—quite in contrast to the traditional view pitting the earthly against the heavenly and the temporal against the eternal. In such a vision of development (as used here the term is not antithetical to "liberation") the human is the route to the divine. The Latin American bishops incorporated this paragraph into the Medellín documents, prefacing it with an explicit reference to Exodus. To strive for full human development today is a form of exodus.

When Gutiérrez speaks of "integral development," he does something similar. He sees the term "liberation" as having "three reciprocally interpenetrating levels of meaning." It means first the aspirations of the poor and in this sense is equivalent to the critique the social theorists make of the notion of "development." At a second level "liberation" refers to the gradual expansion of freedom, understood as the ability of human beings to take charge of their own destiny. At another level "liberation" refers to the freedom of Christ. "The fullness of liberation—a free gift from Christ—is communion with God and with other human beings."

Gutiérrez does not view these as "three parallel or chronologically successive processes" but as "three levels of meaning of a single complex process, which finds its deepest sense and its full realization in the saving work of Christ." Even small, modest actions for liberation, such as the efforts of a village to organize, are part of a much larger movement—ultimately, humankind's exodus toward God.

This theme of "integral liberation" recurs frequently in liberation theology, far more often in fact than questions of Marxism or violence, for example. As ethereal as it might seem, this question does have practical implications. The most important is perhaps that one cannot simply circumscribe a self-contained "religious" sphere to which the church should confine its efforts. Rather the church and Christians should be involved in human history—the one human history—where people are shaping their destiny.

6. CAPTIVITY AND HOPE

Shifting Contexts of Liberation Theology

WHEN THE FIRST SKETCHES OF LIBERATION THEOLOGY APpeared in the late 1960s and early 1970s, several ways to basic structural change in society seemed possible. Guerrilla movements were operating in several countries, although the failure and death of Che Guevara in Bolivia in 1967 seemed to be an omen. The 1970 election victory of Salvador Allende and the openly socialistic Popular Unity coalition held out hope that a sufficiently organized electorate could prevail and achieve deep change in a gradual and nonviolent manner. Similar coalitions were organized for elections in Venezuela and Uruguay. In Argentina some thought that the left should work within Peronism, since the masses were Peronist. Through educational and organizational work within the movement, workers could make Peronism serve their own real interests and thus become a force that was both radical and strong. Finally, the programs of the Peruvian military government that took power in a 1968 coup and called itself revolutionary held out the possibility of alliances with younger, progressive military officers.

"The revolutionary process in Latin America is in full swing," proclaimed the delegates at the Christians for Socialism conference in Santiago in 1972, caught up in the enthusiastic Chilean atmosphere. They would have been more accurate had they pointed to a counterrevolutionary process. Military coups ushered in repressive governments in Brazil (1964), Bolivia (1971), Uruguay (1973), Chile (1973), and Argentina (1976). Moreover, existing military governments shifted rightward in Peru (1975) and Ecuador (1976). Repressive military rule continued in Paraguay and most of Central America. Only in Mexico, Colombia, Venezuela, and Costa Rica did the mechanisms of formal democracy remain and even those governments were capable of utilizing harsh repression.

While details varied from country to country, the new military dictatorships had certain common traits. They were not old-style personal dictatorships but represented rule by the armed forces as institutions. They were a response to the growing grass-roots militancy of the 1960s, which the military saw as "chaos." They sought to legitimize themselves by claiming that only in such regimes could the economy properly develop, and pointed for evidence to the high growth rates of the "Brazilian miracle" of the early 1970s.

Although some saw the new military governments as merely the logical response of the United States and local oligarchies to growing popular movements, and as transitory phenomena, others believed that they constituted a new model of society, a "national security state" with its own coherent ideology. By crushing labor unions, controlling the press, abolishing or neutralizing congresses, and exalting the army, they seemed to merit the label of "dependent fascism."

For a number of years—certainly from the time of the coup in Chile until the end of the decade—the military governments seemed destined to hold power indefinitely. Their violation of elemental human rights posed a direct challenge to the churches.

Backlash in the Hierarchy

In the meantime, there was something of a coup within the Latin American Catholic hierarchy. After the Medellín conference the new pastoral and theological ideas spread rapidly throughout the continent. Each year hundreds of priests and sisters were taking courses in CELAM's own training courses. The general postcouncil attitude of questioning sometimes led to public confrontations between priests' groups and the bishops. A backlash in the hierarchy was inevitable.

The bishops, however, could not simply reverse their position, since the Medellín documents were official church teaching. Those who were uneasy with what was happening needed an alternate framework of social analysis and theology. That need began to be met in 1971 when the Belgian Jesuit Roger Vekemans arrived in Bogotá. During his many years in Chile Vekemans had been a key figure in the developmentalist phase and was closely associated with the Christian Democrats. Indeed, he boasted of channeling $5 million from the CIA to them during the 1964 election campaign. In Bogotá Vekemans set up a research center and in collaboration with the young, shrewd, and ambitious Bishop Alfonso López Trujillo began to publish a journal, *Tierra Nueva,* whose clear purpose was not only to attack liberation theology but to propose an alternate kind of social analysis and theology.

At the same time, López Trujillo and others began a carefully planned effort to capture the machinery of CELAM. López cultivated contacts in the Vatican and among Latin American bishops. In November 1972 these efforts were crowned with success when López Trujillo was elected secretary-general of CELAM. He lost no time in cleaning house, collapsing the several CELAM training institutes into one, which was located in Colombia where he could watch it. The CELAM agencies dealing with missions, media, liturgy, catechetics, etc., became a platform for the attack on liberation theology.

Nevertheless, there were contrary developments even in the Vatican. Pope Paul VI's 1971 encyclical *Octogesima Adveniens* showed the impact of liberation theology. Taking note of the growing interest in socialism among Catholics, the pope refrained from issuing condemnations and simply urged caution and discernment. The same year a worldwide synod of bishops held in Rome recognized that efforts for justice are a "constitutive dimension" of preaching the gospel. Such action, which they explicitly called "liberation," was thus central—not peripheral—to what the church was about. A synod on evangelization held in 1984 reiterated the point.

Thus, at the very time that liberation theology was provoking controversy in Catholicism, some of its central tenets were becoming official church positions.

Holding On to Hope in an Hour of Darkness

Although repressive governments set the tone during the 1970s, events did not unfold in a strictly parallel fashion and conditions varied from one country to another. For example, from 1968 to 1975, precisely the most repressive period of military rule in Brazil, Peru's military seemed to be attempting a new nationalist path to development. In most countries, however, violation of human rights forced the Catholic church to face the consequences of some of the commitments made at Medellín.

The most important development within the church during this period was the quiet, steady growth of base communities.

They provided a space in which people could meet in an atmosphere of respect and reaffirm their own faith and hope. Where the media were censored and intimidated and where governments and armies imposed their ideology of national security, the base communities provided a small space where the truth could be spoken, even if guardedly. In a situation that seemed to offer no human reason for believing things could be different, their message was that things had to change. They became a space where poor people could "speak their word" and where they heard that God was on their side, just as in the time of the Israelites and in the age of the apostles.

Such quiet work could nevertheless provoke a violent response. Typically, church representatives came under attack because they were defending poor people who were victims of abuse. In Brazil repression had been heavy since 1968, especially in the poverty-stricken Northeast. When a young priest-collaborator of Archbishop Helder Cámara of Recife was murdered in 1969, no serious investigation followed. Other priests in rural areas were arrested, jailed, tortured, or expelled. For years newpapers were prohibited from mentioning Archbishop Helder Cámara. Bishops' documents were not allowed to be published. Yet by 1973 the church, and in particular the bishops, were emerging as clear public opponents not only of human rights abuses but of the human consequences of Brazil's approach to development.

In Chile the brutality of the Pinochet coup (1973) provoked a wide-ranging response. Parishes set up soup kitchens and aid projects for the many people who saw their incomes decline drastically as Pinochet reversed the economic direction of the Allende years. An official archdiocesan agency supervised this work and documented and denounced human rights abuses.

In Bolivia, Uruguay, and Paraguay church involvement in human rights activities led to serious conflict with governments. Some incidents were national in scope, while others often remained local. In Latin America as a whole, between 1964 and 1978, 41 priests were killed (6 as guerrilla combatants) and 11 "disappeared." In addition, some 485 were arrested, 46 were tortured, and 253 were expelled from countries. In Argentina in 1976 Bishop Enrique Angelelli was killed in an auto accident that later turned out to have been murder.

How systematic and deliberate these attacks could be became clear in a leaked 1975 document of the Bolivian government under General Hugo Banzer. The "Banzer Plan" laid down procedures for discrediting progressive church leaders and dividing the church. Archbishop Jorge Manrique of La Paz was one of the targets. Suggested tactics included planting subversive documents on church premises. Censoring or closing church papers and radio stations was suggested. This plan was later endorsed by some ten Latin American governments that sent delegations to the meeting of the Latin American Anti-Communist Confederation at its 1977 meeting.

Theological Deepening

During the 1970s the theologians sought to develop the implications of what had been sketched out in the early essays and first books of liberation theology. Since this was not simply a new theological issue but a new way of going about theology, it was logical that the methodology itself should become a topic of reflection. Two recurring questions were how to use the social sciences in theology and how Latin American preoccupations and methodology were different from existing European theology. In 1978 Clodovis Boff published *Teologia e Prática* (Theology and Practice), which seeks to clarify the epistemological status of the new Latin American theology.

Latin American scholars began to work on rediscovering their own church history. Enrique Dussel had led the way with his outline history, and he became the general coordinator of an ambitious projected thirteen-volume history of the church in Latin America. Dussel also wrote several volumes of a philosophy of liberation.

Hugo Assmann had early pointed to the need for a Latin American Christology. Leonardo Boff's *Jesus Christ Liberator* and Jon Sobrino's *Christology at the Crossroads* and Hugo Echegaray's *The Practice of Jesus* began to meet that need. In all three the Latin American dimension may be seen in the concern to see the liberating implications of Jesus' human life, his words and deeds, set in the conflictive circumstance of the time rather than focusing simply on classical questions such as how Jesus can be both divine and human. In the early 1980s Juan Luis Segundo began to publish a multivolume study of Jesus.

Theologians believed that one of their tasks was to critique the ideologies used to justify society as it is. Already in 1968 Bishop Cândido Padín of Brazil had written an essay critiquing the "national security doctrine" of the Brazilian military, and in 1971 Hugo Assmann had examined the military's utilization of Christian symbols to justify itself. Joseph Comblin, a Belgian theologian who had worked in Brazil and Chile since 1958, prepared a systematic theological critique of national security ideology, examining the works of theorists such as the Brazilian General Golbery do Couto e Silva.

A more radical kind of ideological critique was developed by Hugo Assmann and Franz Hinkelammert and others at a small research center in Costa Rica. In his major work, *The Ideological Weapons of Death*, Hinkelammert used Marx's analysis of fetishism in order to unmask the hidden "spirit" of capitalism. He examined social theorists from Max Weber to Milton Friedman, exponents of Catholic "social doctrine," and even the writings of the Trilateral Commission. While relatively few might persevere through Hinkelammert's whole argument, some of this school's central theses soon became popularized. It became common to refer to liberation theology as a theology of life exposing the "theology of death" embodied in capitalism.

▪ ▪ ▪

Puebla

Originally scheduled to coincide with the tenth anniversary of the Medellín meeting, the Puebla conference seemed to provide Bishop López Trujillo and his allies, including some Vatican officials, with the ideal occasion for delegitimizing liberation theology and the kind of pastoral work associated with it. Part of their strategy was to propose an alternate vocabulary and set of symbols, which themselves contained a different interpretation. A preparatory document which the CELAM staff sent the bishops in 1977 described Latin America as in transition from underdevelopment to development—that is, the crisis was one of transition rather than a struggle for liberation from oppression. Bishops' conferences rather roundly rejected this document primarily because of its abstractness and its insensitivity to their pastoral problems. Added to the second working draft was a long appendix outlining about a dozen errors of liberation theology, seemingly setting it up for condemnation. The Vatican and López Trujillo chose many conservative (mainly nonvoting) delegates; no liberation theologians were invited.

Pope Paul VI's death and the five-week papacy of Pope John Paul I had the effect of postponing the conference until early 1979. During the days prior to the conference Pope John Paul II toured Mexico, donning sombreros and giving a first taste of his populist style. Journalists following him thought they heard condemnations of liberation theology.

The Puebla meeting may be seen as a clash between three mind-sets among the bishops. On one side were conservatives who stressed hierarchical authority and doctrinal orthodoxy and were consciously combating liberation theology for what they saw as its Marxism. At the other extreme was a group that might be called liberationists, whose stress was on base communities and who insisted that the church must take on a style of life in keeping with its role of service. They denounced not only abuses but the structures that caused them, and sometimes the capitalist system as such. Both these groups represented minority tendencies. The largest group might be called centrist and was most concerned with church unity. With the conservatives this group shared a concern for church authority, and with the liberationists a conviction about the need to defend human rights, at least in extreme circumstances. These centrist figures played a leading role in leading the conference itself while conservatives and liberationists lobbied, changing wording, adding to some passages, objecting to others.

The massive final document that emerged was inconclusive. Liberationists were grateful that there were no condemnations. The document even used occasional strong language to denounce existing injustices. The overall tone remained developmentalist. For example, the bishops frequently called for greater "participation and communion" in church and society. These words were clearly part of a new kind of church discourse aimed at replacing liberation terminology. Each of the three tendencies could find positive elements. What Puebla called the "preferential option for the poor" was probably the most positive element for the liberationist side. A glaring lack was any direct reference to people being killed for fidelity to their Christian conviction. Conservatives could also find many quotable phrases and whole themes, especially the frequent condemnations of Marxism and violence, and the assertion of hierarchical authority. Centrists could point to the insistence on the properly "religious" role of the church.

Since three types of analysis and theology coexisted in the Puebla document itself, it was clear that tensions would continue within the church.

▪ ▪ ▪

Revolution, "Democratization," Deepening Crisis

As the Puebla meeting was unfolding, the Latin American context was about to shift again. A half year later a broad grassroots movement led by the Sandinista National Liberation Front (FSLN) overthrew the Somoza dictatorship in Nicaragua and the first revolutionary government in Latin America for twenty years took power. Similar revolutionary movements were brewing in El Salvador and Guatemala.

In hindsight, the reasons for revolution in Central America are clear. The existing model of development was exacerbating the already difficult living conditions of people. Governments responded with increased repression to the point where many people felt they had little to lose by supporting insurgencies. The small size of these countries meant that the insurgencies could become nationwide movements.

Having neglected Central America during the 1970s, at the end of the decade the United States turned all its energy into stopping revolution by propping up the Salvadoran regime and creating a counterrevolutionary army to attack Nicaragua.

One of the sources of the new militancy during the 1970s was the church's pastoral work in base communities. At the village level these communities were often a fruitful starting point for the new popular organizations. Church leaders played an important role in defending human rights, especially Archbishop Oscar Romero of El Salvador, who became known as the "voice of the voiceless."

Theologically speaking, the most novel situation was that of Nicaragua. In contrast with the Cuban experience, Christians had played important roles in the antidictatorial struggle. What should their role be in a revolutionary process?

Some church people were soon convinced that, whatever

they might say, the Sandinistas were Marxists and the only proper role for the church was resistance. Yet there were others who believed that the revolution offered the possibility of a more human life for the poor majority of Nicaraguans and that Christians should therefore support it, although not uncritically.

Contrary to the fears of domino theorists, revolution did not spread from Central America to other countries—not because of vigorous U.S. policy but because the larger countries are more diversified and complex. Revolutionary conditions did not develop. By the mid-1980s military dictatorships were giving way to elected civilian governments.

In Brazil from 1975 onward the army slowly orchestrated first a lessening of tensions and then the slow opening of the political process. The press and political parties became active, and many exiles returned. Only in 1985 did an elected civilian government, headed by President José Sarney, take office. Humiliated in its calamitous war with Britain over the Malvinas/Falkland islands, the Argentine army was forced to withdraw from politics. Uruguay, Peru, Bolivia, Ecuador, and Honduras also returned to civilian rule. As part of its regional strategy the United States coaxed the military of El Salvador to allow elections, and for its own reasons the Guatemalan military returned to civilian rule through an election in late 1985.

To what extent was this genuine democracy? Certainly, political parties, congresses, the press, and organizations representing interest groups once more had a role to play in political life. While this might represent an improvement over arbitrary and often brutal military control, it was largely the urban and middle-class sectors that could reenter the political game. The real concerns of the rural peasantry and the poor of the shantytowns were not taken into account in this return to a limited form of democracy. Moreover, violence and repression were still a fact of life. The new civilian governments were powerless to bring to justice those responsible for crimes during the military dictatorship, except in a token way in Uruguay, and in Argentina, where the military had been totally discredited by losing a war. Landholders in Brazil could still have peasants and Indians—and even priests—murdered with impunity.

Far more important than the shift to civilian rule was the deepening economic crisis manifested especially in the massive foreign debt. During the 1970s Latin American governments had borrowed many billions of dollars, primarily from commercial banks rather than from international lending institutions, often in order to finance ambitious infrastructure projects. The world recession at the end of the decade meant lowered demand for their exports. At the same time, policy decisions in the United States raised interest rates. In 1982 the fact that oil-rich Mexico could not pay its debt on schedule raised the specter of a default, which could even cause the collapse of major U.S. banks. In that instance Mexico was able to reschedule its payments, as Argentina and Brazil did in the following two years, but the debt was clearly a long-range problem. By the mid-1980s Latin American countries had to devote approximately 40 percent of their export earnings to service the debt.

Dissatisfaction with the economic effects of military rule—affecting even the middle class—was a major factor in the shift toward civilian rule. Civilians could now share some of the blame. By the same token, the debt may protect the civilian governments from another round of military coups, since the armed forces are aware that they have no solution to the economic crisis.

It is conceivable that the debt will become a focal point for the church. In August 1985 the Cuban government hosted a meeting of some twelve hundred delegates from all over Latin America and representing a broad spectrum of positions. Some one hundred of the participants were Catholic priests. During his closing address Premier Fidel Castro read a message to the conference from Cardinal Paulo Evaristo Arns of São Paulo which stated that it was no longer possible for the debts to be paid and that Latin American governments' most basic commitments were to their people, not to their creditors. Arns' words received a prolonged standing ovation.

Vatican Actions

Within the Catholic church the context also shifted after 1979. On each of his major trips to Latin America (Brazil, 1980; Central America, 1983; and the Andean countries, 1985), Pope John Paul II made enough speeches to fill a small book. While he seemed to be attacking some of the ideas of liberation theology, he also denounced injustice.

More important than the text of the pope's words, however, was the 1983 photo of him shaking his finger at Ernesto Cardenal, the Nicaraguan priest-poet and minister of culture, warning him in effect to normalize his situation (resign his post in the government). In that same stop the pope engaged in a shouting match with people in the crowd attending his mass. According to one version, it was a deliberate Sandinista plot to insult and humiliate the pope. By another account, the people wanted the pope to say something about the actions of the anti-Sandinista *contras,* in particular a word of consolation to the families of seventeen youths whose funeral had been held in the same spot. Ignoring their pleas, the pope urged Catholics to rally around the bishops. He seemed to be endorsing Archbishop Miguel Obando y Bravo's (political) opposition to the Sandinista government. When people began to chant "We want peace!" he shouted back "Silence!" three times.

However the incident actually began, what people remembered was a head-on clash between Pope John Paul II and the Sandinista government (joined by those Christians involved in the revolution). The Vatican continued to put pressure on the priests in government to resign. In 1985 one of them asked for laicization, and Fernando Cardenal was forced to resign from the Jesuits. Both Foreign Minister Miguel D'Escoto and Ernesto Cardenal were suspended from the priesthood.

In the meantime, the Vatican also pressured liberation theologians. In 1983 Cardinal Joseph Ratzinger, the head of the

Vatican's Sacred Congregation for the Doctrine of the Faith, sent the Peruvian bishops a letter listing objections to Gustavo Gutiérrez' theology. Even under Vatican urging the Peruvian bishops were deadlocked over whether they could condemn Gutiérrez. Gutiérrez was even called to Rome for private consultation with Vatican officials.

The Vatican took a different tack with the Brazilian Franciscan Leonardo Boff. His book *Church: Charism and Power* contains some of the sharpest and most specific criticisms of the Catholic church system to come from Latin America. Rather than going through the Brazilian bishops, who would have supported him, Ratzinger first called Boff to Rome for a discussion in September 1984. Two Brazilian cardinals accompanied him to show the hierarchy's support. In March 1985 the Vatican issued a document answering Boff's criticisms and then in May 1985 prohibited him from publishing or teaching for an indefinite period. In the meantime, Cardinal Ratzinger had published an "Instruction" on liberation theology, which, under the guise of drawing attention to some errors, amounted to an attack (see Chapter Twelve).

There were strong indications that this was indeed a systematic atack by the Vatican aimed at delegitimizing liberation theology in all its forms. Such a view would square with Pope John Paul II's own Polish view of Marxism as inevitably in conflict with the church. It also seemed to fit with what some saw as a long-range program by the pope and Ratzinger aimed at "restoration"—that is, an attempt to return to some of the pre-Vatican II hierarchical discipline and control that had been lost after the council. There was something of a neoconservative backlash in the churches, expressed in movements such as Comunione e Liberazione and Opus Dei, a highly disciplined and secret society of Catholic professional people.

In the end, the Vatican's appointment of bishops might turn out to be more decisive than papal statements. If John Paul II left in place a generation of bishops reflecting his own mindset, the impact might be far-reaching (comparable to the legacy of judicial appointments during the Reagan administration).

Nevertheless, there were some countervailing trends. During his 1983 visit to Central America the pope urged "dialogue" (i.e., negotiations) in El Salvador, visited Archbishop Romero's tomb, and embraced Indians in Guatemala (where the government had slaughtered tens of thousands of them). In his encyclical on human work, *Laborem Exercens,* the pope took positions that could be seen to be at least in dialogue with Marxism. Parallel to the themes that seemed to question liberation theology, there were continual references to injustice and to the rights of human beings. In April 1986 the Vatican issued an "Instruction on Christian Freedom and Liberation" which took a more benign—though highly abstract—view of liberation theology. That same month the Brazilian bishops had a cordial three-day meeting with Pope John Paul II and Vatican officials, and the silence imposed on Leonardo Boff was lifted.

In short, the ecclesiastical context remained fluid or ambiguous. Most important, the future of liberation theology would depend not so much on intentions—the popes', the bishops', or the theologians'—as on events themselves.

7. THE INFINITE WORTH OF THE POOR

A Critical Vision of Human Rights

In 1976 the Guatemalan bishops issued a pastoral letter that began speaking about reconstruction after the earthquake that had killed twenty-two thousand people and left one hundred thousand homeless. It then went on to address the general condition of the country.

For over ten years death squads (made up largely of army and police) had been murdering hundreds of citizens a year with impunity. Hundreds a year were abducted and disappeared. Public protest was limited to vague newspaper hand-wringing over "violence."

That the bishops themselves had said little was due in great measure to Cardinal Mario Casariego, who openly defended the government and the army and stymied the efforts of priests and even his fellow bishops who were concerned. Taking advantage of his absence from the country, the other bishops spoke in terms that were unusually specific for Guatemala. They pointed to the frequent assassination attempts and declared that murder was becoming "a business. Indeed, many who commit such a crime believe they are serving their country, and that they are even defending Western Christian civilization." The bishops said there was no justification for the "armed groups" roaming the country "kidnapping and murdering citizens in a permanent climate of terror."

I find one passage from their letter, which did not attract immediate attention, a remarkable statement of the underlying theological rationale for church involvement in the defense of human rights.

> The human being—every human being—is
> —God's beloved creature,
> —made to his image and likeness,
> —endowed with intelligence and will
> and therefore called to be free and live in community.
>
> Moreover, every human being is called by Christ to grow, so as to become a sharer in the divine nature, and thus reach full realization in God. This is the source of the immense dignity of the human person. Therefore, every human being should have the very same opportunities for his or her development, and likewise be responsible for the same duties and obligations.
>
> Hence,
> —the most humble of all Guatemalans,
> —the most exploited and outcast,
> —the sickest and most unschooled,
> is worth more than all the wealth of the country, and is sacred and untouchable.

Out of context these words seem rather doctrinal. What made them radical was the fact that they were uttered in a country where in fact wealth and the wealthy do have the last word. To take but one example, every year in Guatemala hundreds of people are intoxicated because of pesticide use far above recommended levels, with no regard for farm workers and their families. Dozens of deaths a year are reported, but the true number is higher since doctors are under pressure not to blame deaths on pesticides. The bishops are saying that each individual peasant—those the landowners treat as a disposable labor supply—is worth more than the plantation, indeed worth more than all the plantations and businesses in Guatemala.

Seen theologically, to affirm the infinite worth of each person is a proclamation of the gospel, of "good news to the poor." In this sense the defense of human dignity and human rights is not an optional function but essential and central to the church's mission of evangelizing.

As I will discuss below, in the 1970s Latin American theologians were critical of conventional notions of human rights. Nevertheless, it is important to note that the church resisted the most flagrant human rights abuses of repressive governments.

One of the church's major services was simply to provide a "space" for people to come together, support one another, and renew their hope and faith when nothing on the horizon offered hope. For example, a base community might discuss the gospel account in which the disciples, frightened and despairing on a storm-tossed sea, see Jesus walking over the waters toward them. Their interpretation might be that Jesus continues to accompany his followers even in the midst of dangers and storms today. People might feel no need to explicitly identify government repression as the "storm."

At the official level bishops did not immediately respond to the shift to repressive governments. Some Brazilian bishops welcomed the 1964 coup, for example. Gradually, however, often spurred by the arrest, torture, expulsion, or murder of church personnel, bishops began to take stands. For example, in 1976 the Brazilian bishops drew attention to "arbitrary acts and terrorisms: indiscriminate repression, persecutions, informing, armed groups, para-police, arrest, prison, expulsion, disappearances, abductions, torture, deaths, murders." They continued: "Let us not confuse true peace with the silence that is imposed by a fear of arbitrary repression. We do not want a peace of cemeteries, but a peace that defends life, in all its aspects, physical as well as moral." Such general language has bite only if the public understands the words as aimed at identifiable groups. In an earlier statement the bishops had in fact used the term "death squads."

Taken altogether, the bishops' conferences of the twenty-odd Latin American countries have produced hundreds of statements on social questions from the late 1960s onward. A major theme has been human rights.

Individual bishops could be much more specific and concrete than a national bishops' conference. The most outstanding example was Archbishop Oscar Romero of San Salvador, who, in his Sunday sermons from 1977 onward, addressed the problems of violence in his country. It was undoubtedly his denunciation of human rights violations by official Salvadoran troops that prompted his murder in March 1980.

Bishops did not always take a vigorous stand. In Argentina during the "dirty war" of the late 1970s, the bishops were notably silent even though at least one bishop and some ten priests were murdered. It was the Madres de Mayo, the mothers and family members of the disappeared, who challenged the military, while the bishops temporized and some even made promilitary statements. When the armed forces withdrew to their barracks after their humiliating defeat in the Malvinas-Falklands War, the Catholic hierarchy had lost credibility.

Besides making statements, the institutional church has supported human rights groups, thus affording them some protection. In Chile and El Salvador the official church itself formed agencies to monitor and document human rights abuses. In Chile the church's Vicariate of Solidarity worked with international aid agencies to set up soup kitchens and small-scale development projects in parishes in order to offset the economic damage of the Pinochet government's policies, which drastically impoverished the working classes.

As the initial quote from the Guatemalan bishops indicates, the human rights activity of the church is rooted in a theology.

In fact, one could say that the actions of repressive governments are also rooted in an implicit theology, one which has some support in the church's historical alliance with ruling classes. Joseph Comblin notes that the image of God held by authoritarian rulers is "the state, the nation, order, power, law." By contrast, in Christianity "God's image is the human being, the ordinary man or woman of the street."

Comblin also points out that in national security systems love is regarded as what binds citizens together, like soldiers in an army. It means "friendship toward friends, hostility toward enemies." When the secret police are after someone, all that person's erstwhile friends disappear. The biblical words for "love," on the other hand, mean "fidelity to one's word and loyalty to others." An authoritarian society makes Christian love impossible.

These are simply examples of a theologian uncovering the implicit "theology"—or "antitheology"—of regimes that massively violate human rights.

Critical Vision of Human Rights

A number of Latin American theologians were wary of the stress on human rights during the 1970s, and they were concerned about the way the church might respond. Focusing simply on the worst cases—torture and death squads—might support the notion that these were the "abuses" of perverse individuals or groups and hence obscure the fact that they were carried out to protect the interests of local privileged elites, and ultimately U.S. hegemony. Moreover, the church tended to react most when its own personnel were affected (e.g., when a priest was expelled) or when the suppression of civil and political liberties reached the middle classes, and ignore the more systematic abuse of the very poor. In other words, to simply accept the

Western liberal definition of human rights, with its individualistic thrust, was a trap.

Such suspicions were heightened when the Carter administration (1977–81) made human rights the ostensible centerpiece of its foreign policy, at least with regard to the Third World. It was at this time that the Trilateral Commission began to attract attention. Established in 1973 at the initiative of David Rockefeller, the Trilateral Commission is a think tank that brings together elite figures from business, government, and communications from the United States, Europe, and Japan to elaborate more coordinated and rational approaches to global problems, from trade to environmental pollution. Many high-level Carter officials, such as Zbigniew Brzezinski, were members. Although the Trilateral Commission's approach to the Third World was clearly more liberal and accommodating than that of the Nixon-Ford era (1969–77), Latin Americans saw it primarily as a means of making imperial domination function more smoothly. That was true even of its ostensible advocacy of human rights.

Hugo Assmann, Franz Hinkelammert, and others at DEI (Ecumenical Research Department) in San José, Costa Rica, devoted considerable attention to these issues. In 1978 they published a two-volume set of readings entitled *Carter y la Lógica del Imperialismo* (Carter and the Logic of Imperialism), collecting writings by Latin Americans and North Americans. Some of the essay titles reveal the direction of their critique of human rights: "Imperialism and Carter's Foreign Policy"; "Whose Human Rights?"; "The Social Dimension of the Right to Live"; "The Defense of Human Rights as Solidarity with the Oppressed"; "The Third World Begins to Create an Alternative Language on Human Rights"; "The Rights of Peoples and the New International Economic Order." In 1978 DEI organized a meeting of social scientists and theologians to reflect on these topics. The papers were collected in another two-volume collection, *Capitalismo: Violencia y Anti-Vida* (Capitalism: Violence and Anti-Life).

Writing on "Human Rights, Evangelization, and Ideology,"

Juan Luis Segundo took a startling position. He said that in principle he was in agreement with the military of his own country, Uruguay, in their rejection of foreign criticism of their human rights abuses—even though he had suffered a degree of violation of his own rights. (According to Amnesty International, by the mid-1970s Uruguay had the highest per capita ratio of political prisoners in the world.) Nevertheless, Segundo asserted that the root of human rights violations was to be found in the impossible conditions laid on Third World countries by the rich countries, conditions which could only be maintained by repression. Hence, it was hypocritical for those countries to then criticize the regimes that carried out the repression. There is an "ideological trap" of seeing sadism and torture as being genetically Latin American. "They accuse us of not being democratic, when it is they who are preventing us from being so."

> Doesn't affirming human rights lead us to maximize, as a violation of freedom of thought or expression, a newspaper being closed or a writer being jailed, and to minimize, as though they were the result of "natural" causes, the economic and social conditions that mean that the population as a whole not only cannot express itself, but that it is deprived of the ability to learn and hence to think?

Rather than develop an elaborate theology of human rights, Latin American theologians pointed to the need to develop an "alternative language." They insisted that one should not speak simply of "human rights" in general but of the "rights of the majorities" or the "rights of the poor" since it was they whose rights were being violated. Such an expression, moreover, is closer to the Bible's image of a God who sides with the poor and against their oppressors.

Latin American theologians also questioned what they saw as "idealist" language about human rights in liberal Western discourse and the failure to realize that some rights are prior to others. They insisted that the most basic right is the right to life and consequently the right to the means of life, that is, employment and land.

Some also questioned the conventional manner of focusing human rights simply on the individual and on the state; they insisted also on the "rights of peoples" and pointed to the "Universal Declaration of the Rights of Peoples" made in Algeria by a congress convoked for that purpose in 1976. This declaration stressed the rights of peoples (which it did not define) to their self-determination, to their natural resources, to the common patrimony of humankind, to a just recompense for their labor, to choose their own economic and social systems, to speak their own language, and so forth. The representatives at that meeting came primarily from revolutionary governments and from national liberation movements.

In a word, these theologians were arguing that rather than simply accept the Western notion of human rights, with its focus on individual rights vis-à-vis the state, which could easily become an ideology masking the daily suffering and death of the poor majority, Latin Americans should develop a new language about human rights. That language should express the subsistence rights of the poor majority of humankind, including their collective rights as peoples.

Critique of National Security Ideology

At first, the wave of military coups from 1964 onward could be seen as a transitory phenomenon, the reaction of privileged groups to the growing militancy of the 1960s. As military governments came to be the norm, however, many began to conclude that what was appearing was a new model of regime. Some spoke of "dependent fascism." The most common term was the "national security state."

U.S. policy contributed toward this shift. After the Rio Treaty

(1947) the United States provided Latin American armed forces with a new rationale, anticommunism, and during the 1960s it turned them into counterinsurgency forces. The "enemy" was no longer external but internal. The United States was involved in the coups in both Brazil and Chile, and in a more general sense, U.S. training no doubt contributed toward awakening the vocation to politics among generals and colonels throughout Latin America. When civilian government seemed to falter, they were ready to step in.

As early as 1968 Bishop Cândido Padín of Brazil pointed to the existence of an explicit ideology of national security. During the 1970s Comblin spelled it out and critiqued it in some detail. As articulated in books by Generals Golbery do Couto e Silva (Brazil), Jorge Atencio (Argentina), and Augusto Pinochet (Chile), national security views "geopolitics" as occupying a central place within human knowledge. (It was also central to Nazi and fascist ideologies.) Geopolitics holds that individuals and groups must be subordinate to the state, which it views as a kind of organism and as the ultimate source of values. There is a basic Hobbesian assumption that all states are permanently at war with one another, although they may enter alliances against common enemies. The whole art of governance is understood as synonymous with strategy; the highest good is national security. Even economic growth is first justified in terms of security. The welfare of citizens is subordinate to security, although it is admitted that beyond a certain point unmet needs themselves threaten security if they generate unrest.

The agents of development are elites, both military and technocratic. Bishop Padín points out that in national security doctrine only these elites are regarded as mature. The remaining groups in the nation, including peasants, labor unions, and university students and faculty, are seen as minors still needing tutelage. He sees this attitude as a continuation of the attitude of the colonizers toward the conquered population.

Another assumption of national security doctrine is that the nation is allied with the United States in the East-West conflict. Religion is seen from this perspective. Western Christian civilization is threatened by Marxist atheism in the East. National security governments expect the church to be an ally, and they are prepared to provide favors as long as the church carries out its appointed role. They also expect the church to agree with their public moralistic stands, whether in clamping down on pornography or limiting political dissent.

Comblin critiques the tenets of national security ideology in considerable detail. First, he questions the notion of a "Christian civilization," which for national security ideologues is merely a cultural phenomenon, "a collection of beliefs and ritual patterns, laws and traditions." In no sense do they have in mind the awakening of freedom, which is the essence of evangelization. He also takes up the military's argument that the church should join with them in a crusade against "atheistic" communism, insisting that it is contradictory to fight atheism with violence. True knowledge of God is found not in using the right words—including the word "God"—but in love. ("Anyone who says 'I know him,' and does not keep his commandments, is a liar" [1 John 2:4].)

National security ideologies make assumptions about human nature, freedom, and the state that are at odds with Christianity. Human life is assumed to be an unending struggle, indeed a war, in which other people are either allies or enemies. Permanently insecure in this war, individuals must find refuge in power. Only the state can create order; people must pay for security by giving up freedom.

Comblin counters with the gospel's assertion that Christ has come to bring peace and its command that enemies must be loved. Love of enemy relativizes "the criterion of security." The Holy Spirit has come to make these things possible. "Human beings *are* able to create peace and justice. They must not give up such a task to the state."

For the most part, these ideologies ignore freedom, which is central to a biblical view of life. For instance, freedom entails getting "rid of the slave who dwells within oneself," including "the slavery of the need for security." It means claiming the right to be a person, not an inanimate object, in society. Freedom is attained only through "free associations, free agreements, free covenants." In all these respects the Christian sense of freedom runs counter to national security ideology.

Comblin finds that theology has tended to ignore the state, or to fall into an easy naiveté and optimism with regard to it. Fundamental to a biblical view is a distinction between the people and the state. States are relative; they are meant to serve. "States pass; the people remain." The state should create the conditions of freedom.

> The only good power is a limited power; there must be laws and principles above it and stronger than it. These institutions above the power of the state are the embodiment of the Spirit in history. A political society without such organs to limit the power of the state cannot possibly be a Christian society.

This summary may serve to give an idea of how Comblin draws out the underlying contradictions between the pretensions of national security ideology and biblical Christianity. If the world really is as Golbery and others conceive it, "the Christian message becomes empty and meaningless, except as a utopian document of the past."

I believe this is a particularly illuminating example of liberation theology at work. In responding to the challenge posed by this new form of state and ideology, theologians not only undermined the ability of states to justify their violence against the people, but in so doing they uncovered a further depth of meaning in the Bible and Christian tradition.

At Puebla the bishops outlined national security doctrine as an ideology, alongside "capitalist liberalism" and "Marxist collectivism," noting that it was used to justify violations of human rights. The bishops said national security doctrine was incompatible with Christianity in its view of both the human being and the state.

By the mid-1980s the military governments had been chastened by economic failure, and in the case of Argentina by military defeat. Only Chile seemed to embody the national security ideology in its purest form. Much of the underlying ideology was still operative, however, even though governments had passed to civilian hands.

Critiquing the Model of Development

In the conventional Western view, defending human rights is essentially a matter of protecting the individual from an arbitrary or unjust state. Beyond physical integrity (the right not to be killed, tortured, or subjected to unusual punishment) the stress is on due process, equality before the law, and on the freedoms of assembly and expression.

Marxists and representatives of the Third World regard this liberal conception of human rights as narrowly individualistic since it ignores or downplays the most basic right, the right to survival and life, a right that is essentially connected to the right to work. In other words, the right to "life, liberty, and the pursuit of happiness" is meaningless to those who live at an inhuman level because they cannot find work or have no land on which to raise food. Freedom of the press is relative in a country where 80 percent of the population cannot afford to buy a newspaper. The liberal countercritique is that, as desirable as they might be, so-called social and economic rights are not rights in the strict sense. Rights to freedom of speech, for example, are clear and enforceable. By contrast, it is not clear on whom the responsibility for employment lies, nor how such a right could be enforced. Note, however, that the 1948 United Nations Universal Declaration of Human Rights does include economic and social rights, as does the most developed Catholic statement on human rights, Pope John XXIII's encyclical *Pacem in Terris*.

Latin American church people are critical of the limitations of Western notions of human rights. They have sought to move beyond denouncing abuses, like torture, abduction, and murder to question the very development model that provides small elites with luxurious lives while the majority live in dehumanizing conditions.

In May 1973 two regional groups of Brazilian bishops issued pastoral letters criticizing the human impact of the high-growth development model of the "Brazilian miracle." The bishops of the Northeast stated that Brazil had taken the route of "dependent associated capitalism" in which development served "not the interests of Brazilian society" but "the profit of foreign companies and their associates in our country." By 1970 the richest 1 percent of the population controlled a greater share of the national income (17 percent) than the bottom half (13.7 percent). The system was making the rich richer and the poor poorer—or as the poor themselves expressed it, "the big fish eats the little one." At that time, when independent voices from the press, labor, and intellectuals had been silenced, to question the course taken by the military government was a form of secular heresy.

In their letter the bishops from the Central West also critiqued the model of development. They called capitalism "the greatest evil, sin accumulated, the rotten root, the tree that produces fruits we have come to know: poverty, hunger, sickness, death." They explicitly called for moving "beyond private property of the means of production (factories, land, trade, banks, credit sources)."

While admitting that they did not know what the kind of world they were calling for would look like, they laid down some elements of a utopian vision:

> We want a world where the fruits of work will belong to everyone.
>
> We want a world where people will work not to get rich but so all will have what they need to live on: food, health care, housing, schooling, clothes, shoes, water, electricity.
>
> We want a world where money will be at the service of human beings and not human beings at the service of money. . . .

> We want a world in which the people will be one, and the division between rich and poor will be abolished. . . .

From the viewpoint of liberation theology a consistent pursuit of human rights leads to the struggle to make basic changes in society itself.

Both the conceptualization and the achievement of human rights have a history. That should be clear to Americans whose founders proclaimed the "self-evident" truth that human beings had inalienable rights, and yet allowed only property-owning white males to vote.

Today's struggle for human rights in Latin America is a contribution to that common—and unfinished—history.

8. TAKING SIDES

Faith, Politics, and Ideology

FEW THINGS ARE MORE OBVIOUS ABOUT THE CATHOLIC CHURCH than its involvement in politics. The Vatican maintains a worldwide diplomatic service. In the United States, pollsters and politicians scrutinize the Catholic vote. Pope John Paul II travels to all continents with messages that are heard in political terms.

Yet the bishops themselves will steadfastly maintain that even in the public sphere their role is religious, not partisan. Vatican II declared that the church "must in no way be confused with the political community, nor bound to any particular system." Understood in historical perspective, that and similar statements are a repudiation of the church's previous preference for governments that officially recognize Catholicism.

Given its majority status, the Catholic church, and particularly the hierarchy, has considerable political weight in Latin

American society. The church can legitimize or delegitimize. Often it cannot evade an issue—silence can be read as implicit consent. The fact that the Argentine bishops did not protest the "dirty war" in which at least nine thousand, and possibly many more, Argentines were murdered made them silent accomplices. Similarly, the Catholic church can scarcely avoid taking some kind of position on the revolution in Nicaragua.

Protestants, on the other hand, are normally under 10 percent of the population, and any particular church will be less than 1 percent. Hence, individual Protestant churches can usually avoid taking a stance on public issues, as can the Roman Catholic church in most of Asia, with the notable exception of the Philippines. Protestant churches in Latin America have a "private" character, while the Catholic church is, willy-nilly, a protagonist in the public sphere.

Here my aim will be to clarify in broad outlines how liberation theologians view politics and its intersection with faith and theology.

Whose Politics?

Liberation theology is often accused of being an unwarranted mixing of religion and politics. Theologians are accused of attempting to use religion on the left, just as conservative elements used the church for centuries. The priests supporting the Sandinista revolution in Nicaragua might seem to be one more variety of court theologians.

In commonsense terms it seems clear that when the pope or others object to the involvement of clergy in politics their real concern is a particular kind of involvement, even though the objection is expressed in terms of general principles. Thus, priests who work with the Sandinista government are suspended, while Cardinal Obando, who denounces the Sandinistas at every opportunity but never denounces the atrocities of the U.S.-supported *contras* and even celebrates mass for their backers in Miami, is cast in the mantle of a prophet. No voices are raised when Cardinal Jaime Sin of Manila actively participates in forging the anti-Marcos election coalition, urges Filipinos to vote and then to defend the election results, and then backs the army officers who turn against Marcos. Was the cardinal supporting an extraordinary surge of nonviolent people's power—or helping the United States and the Filipino elites blunt and co-opt what might have become a real revolution? Whatever the result, it is hard to see it as anything but a use of the church's political power. The same is true of Pope John Paul II, who untiringly states that priests should steer clear of politics, and yet visiting Peru in 1985 can urge the "Shining Path" guerrillas to surrender, although he had made no such recommendation to the U.S.-created and -backed *contras* in Nicaragua two years before. A cynical outsider might conclude that what the pope means is that he will handle the church's political involvement himself.

Some within the church would argue that it is illusory to imagine that one can be above politics. Catholics should accept the fact that the church does have influence and should put that influence on the side of the aspirations of the poor. In negative terms this would mean being careful not to support an unjust present order; in positive terms, it would mean encouraging and supporting the overall thrust of people's movements toward liberation, without being tied to specific organizations or programs.

Official Catholic teaching, however, steadfastly resists such a position. At Vatican II the bishops decared that the church was not wedded to any particular type of regime. They saw political activity as proper to lay people but not to priests, who should be "ministers of unity." Individual Christians are to make their own political options. This image of politics seems to assume basic order in society, a smooth-running Western democracy with a high degree of consensus, in which politics is a game played between competing parties according to agreed-upon rules. In such a case there seems to be little justification for the church advising people on these choices.

Latin American experience has raised questions about this seemingly clear position. Christians who started out trying to apply the church's "social teaching" have tended to become radicalized. They realize that justice will not be achieved without systemic political change. The essential political issue is not which party should occupy a government, when all are operating within the parameters laid down by oligarchical and military elites. It is rather how the rules of the game can be changed so that the poor can themselves become players.

In a 1971 encyclical Pope Paul VI took note that Christians were feeling the need "to pass from economics to politics" and that they were being attracted to socialism and Marxism. While pointing to some dangers, the pope did not issue condemnations but counseled Christians and local communities to use "careful judgement" and "discernment." This relative openness to a critical discernment of socialism and even Marxism was a new element in official Catholic teaching.

At Puebla (1979) the bishops spoke of politics as a "constitutive dimension of human beings which has an all-embracing aspect because its aim is the common welfare of society." The church "feels it has a duty and a right to be present" in politics, inasmuch as "Christianity is supposed to evangelize the whole of human life, including the political dimension." The bishops explicitly rejected the notion that faith should be restricted to personal or family life. Here they were reacting to accusations that in taking positions on human rights violations they were stepping outside their rightful sphere.

At the same time, the Puebla meeting reaffirmed Vatican II's stress on the church's properly religious role and on the distinction between clergy and laity. The bishops made what seemed to be a clear distinction between two meanings of the term "politics." Understood in the broad sense, "politics" means "the pursuit of the common good," and is of concern to the church. As they pursue this common good, however, people form differing groups with different ideologies. "Party politics is properly the realm of lay people." Since pastors "must be concerned with unity," they cannot be involved with "partisan" political ideologies.

At first glance, this distinction seems clear and applicable. Church authorities should not direct people how to vote, for example. However, the deeper questions in Latin America are not about elections as such. The basic confrontation is between the "people," understood as the poor majority and those allied with it, and the present power structure. Often this confrontation is latent or is masked; sometimes it erupts in spontaneous activity; sometimes it is embodied in a movement or a series of movements. When the members of the Mutual Support Group in Guatemala march through the street chanting of their seven hundred "disappeared" loved ones—"They were taken alive; we want them back alive!"—are they defending the common good? Or are they engaged in "partisan" activity? Should the church—specifically the hierarchy—support such a group?

As clear as the distinctions might seem on paper, they do not seem operative in highly conflictive real situations.

Liberation theology tends to take another approach. The theologians insist that faith cannot be neutral when the life and death of the people are in question. Political and ideological choices and options cannot be sidestepped.

A case in point is how Archbishop Oscar Romero dealt with issues related to what were called the "popular organizations." These were mass-based organizations, initially of peasants, that arose in the mid-1970s in El Salvador. The two largest organizations had close connections with church pastoral work in base communities. FECCAS (Federation of Christian Peasants of El Salvador) was originally a Christian Democrat-inspired organization, which became more militant under new leadership. The UTC (Union of Rural Workers) grew directly out of a land invasion in the department of San Vicente in November 1974. Peasants of a base community occupied the unused land, seeking to pressure the owner to rent it to them. The army, fearing the precedent, attacked the group, killing six and jailing twenty-six (thirteen of whom "disappeared"). At that point they organized the UTC. Later on, both groups joined together. By the end of the decade it was clear that these popular organizations were a political arm of the FPL (Popular Liberation Forces) guerrilla organization.

Concientización in base communities prepared the soil for these organizations, which provided a vehicle by which the peasants could become linked on a national level. In the eyes of the peasants there was undoubtedly a rather straight-line evolution from their original *concientización* experience through the church to their militancy in organizations that used a Marxist vocabulary although their methods were nonviolent. (Manilio Argueta's novel *One Day of Life* gives a vivid sense of this process through the eyes of peasants in Chalatenango.)

Landholders denounced these groups as subversives and terrorists and blamed the priests and other church people. In August 1978 four of the Salvadoran bishops issued a formal statement in effect condemning the organizations as "Marxist."

Archbishop Romero took a fundamentally different tack in a pastoral letter called "The Church and the Popular Organizations," published that same month. He defended the peasants' right to organize and pointed out how that right was violated in El Salvador. By making a reference to Vatican II's teaching on politics, the archbishop was implicitly recognizing that these organizations were as legitimate as traditional political parties.

Romero acknowledged that there was a relationship between the church and those organizations that had sprung from its work. The inference seemed to be that priests need not disavow organizations like FECCAS and UTC when they became involved in struggle. He then insisted that although faith and politics are connected they are not the same thing and that the distinction should be maintained. Particular political programs should not replace the content of the faith, nor should the church or its symbols be used on behalf of a particular organization. No one should be compelled to join an organization. Faith should always remain the "ultimate framework of reference" for a Christian. Individuals should not be leaders of the Christian community and a political organization at the same time. An individual who is a leader within a base community and a militant peasant organization should go through a process of discernment and decide which form of leadership is his or her calling. The role of priests is to give guidance in regard to faith and justice, and only in exceptional circumstances, and after informing the bishop, should they take on political tasks.

The peasants saw a clear continuity between their awakening in base communities and their active militancy in national organizations. Romero was both affirming their right to belong to such organizations and cautioning them not to let faith be totally absorbed by politics. What was unusual was Romero's willingness to confront the issues in specific terms. To his death he remained a firm supporter of the popular organizations, which he regarded as a genuine expression of the people's aspirations, without committing the church to supporting particular organizations. Although he took responsibility for this document—along with Bishop Arturo Rivera y Damas, who also signed it—one may reasonably assume that theologians in El Salvador had a hand in its preparation.

Ideologies and Faith

The church, declared Pope John Paul II in his opening address to the Puebla Conference, "does not need to have recourse to ideological systems in order to love, defend, and collaborate in the liberation of the human being." The only inspiration it needs is the message entrusted to it.

At Puebla the bishops defined ideology as "any conception that offers a view of the various aspects of life from the standpoint of a specific group in society." Hence, "every ideology is partial because no one group can claim to identify its aspirations with those of society as a whole." Ideologies are legitimate, but they have a tendency to "absolutize the interests they uphold, the vision they propose, and the strategy they promote," thus becoming "lay religions." The bishops state that "neither the Gospel nor the Church's social teaching deriving from it are ideologies."

The church "accepts the challenge and contribution of ideologies in their positive aspects, and in turn challenges, criticizes and relativizes them." Specifically, the bishops examine "capitalist liberalism," "Marxist collectivism," and the "doctrine of national security." Behind the apparent evenhandedness, clearly what they are most concerned about is Marxism.

In 1978 a group of theologians meeting in Caracas, Venezuela, hoping to contribute to the pre-Puebla debate, had articulated a fundamentally different position. They began by distinguishing three senses of the term "ideology." In a Marxist sense an ideology is used by a dominant class to mask its privileges and interests and is imposed on society as a whole—through the mass media, for example. In this sense ideology denotes "false consciousness." A second meaning is that of an overall philosophy, an all-embracing worldview that seeks to explain the whole of reality. The third sense is much more limited and denotes "a system of means and ends for confronting a particular period in history in its differing and changing circumstances, and for leading history toward goals that are partial and subject to revision."

Church authorities tend to understand ideologies in the second sense, that is, as all-embracing systems that seek to account for everything, while liberation theologians understand them in this third, more limited sense.

Christians cannot be indifferent toward ideologies, continue the Caracas theologians. For millions of people in Latin America they are matters of life and death. If faith in Jesus Christ impels people to find ways of making love effective, they must explore "which systems favor life and which are at the service of death." The time has come to cease striving for neutrality, whether out of hypocrisy or a lack of awareness, to "decisively opt and take sides clearsightedly and responsibly." It is their active involvement in Christian communities that leads these theologians to the conviction that they have to take sides—just as the God of Israel and Jesus Christ takes sides and stands with the poor and the oppressed. The impulse for these options comes from faith.

Furthermore, they observe, such options are not based on the teaching of the hierarchy, nor do they appeal to the church's social teaching as a kind of necessary "bridge" linking faith and Christian praxis. Rather, they see a process of discernment in Christian communities themselves, which are seeking to determine "which systems, which forces, which programs and which groups can be regarded as the concrete bearers of liberation in history."

The church's options have to become incarnate in such efforts and movements; that entails "being ideologized, taking sides, and thus taking flesh and being committed to concrete human history." In effect, these theologians are saying that the church cannot observe the struggle of the people from the sidelines, but must be involved in those movements that embody their aspirations. That does not mean ignoring the philosophy or previous history of such movements (without mentioning it by name they are obviously thinking of Marxism). However, the confrontation between such movements and the faith that motivates Christians to be involved is not a matter of debate or polemics, since both those movements and Christian commitment are to be measured by how faithful they are in practice to the hope of the poor.

Christians who make such options have to give up the aim of always being right. "Only someone who sticks to the area of general ethical principles can always be right." Such an approach to the truth, through sharing risk and struggle, is difficult for the hierarchy, accustomed as it is to thinking of itself as possessing the truth.

In a word, these theologians are saying that Christians and the church itself must make an option for an ideology, understood as what Latin Americans call a *proyecto* ("project"). A "project" in this sense is not simply a far-off and unrealizable utopia, nor is it a short-run program. It is something in between, something like the overall thrust of society. In that sense, socialism is such a possible "project" understood not as a mythical classless society, but as a possible alternative embracing a basic shift in power relations whereby the poor majority become real actors in society, and a series of structural reforms (land reform and a general reorientation of the means of production to serve the basic needs of the majority).

Bishops tend to say that the church cannot choose between competing ideologies. In explanation they may say, for example, that the church has "opted for the Risen Christ."

The Caracas theologians, and others like them, insist that having an ideology is part of the human condition. One cannot avoid ideology any more than one can avoid breathing air or speaking in sentences. (At one point in the Puebla meeting Bishop Germán Schmitz of Peru challenged his fellow bishops: "Let him who is without ideology cast the first stone.") The important distinction is between uncritical and even unconscious acceptance of existing ideologies.

The End of Christendom?

As noted at the outset of this chapter, from a commonsense viewpoint, the question seems simple: will the church and Christians take their stand with the existing power structure or with those struggling for change. However, Pablo Richard, a Chilean theologian exiled since 1973, argues that what is really occurring is a crisis of "christendom."

"Christendom" refers to that period when the church seemed to be coterminous with society as a whole, most notably during the Middle Ages. In christendom there are dual powers, temporal and spiritual: Christianity receives official recognition and in return supplies religious legitimation for those who hold temporal power.

In modern theology "christendom" has a negative connotation. The cost of official recognition by Constantine was compromise with wealth and power. The secularizing trend of recent centuries and the church's consequent loss of power is purifying. When society itself no longer reinforces Christian tradition, people can live their faith out of conviction rather than convention.

Richard interprets the history of the Catholic church in Latin America in terms of a christendom. It is obvious enough that the Iberian conquerors set up a form of christendom in the colonies. Colonial christendom was destroyed during the struggle for independence and its aftermath through the nineteenth century, but church leaders never gave up their hope of reestablishing christendom. Many initiatives of the first half of the twentieth century, and particularly Christian Democratic parties and related organizations, can be seen as efforts to set up a "neo-christendom."

Starting around 1960 the whole idea of even a "neo-christendom" is in crisis, asserts Richard. The overall crisis of Latin American society points toward a new kind of society being born. Within the church itself there are now groups, particularly those identified as the "popular church," who reject any kind of christendom formula. What is in crisis, in other words, is not the church as such, but a particular model of church-state relations. If the overall people's movement leads to a new kind of society, there will be a new kind of church-state relationship, one that moves beyond any kind of christendom. If, on the other hand, authoritarian military regimes prevail, the result will be a new "military-ecclesiastical christendom."

One of the suggestive points of this rather sweeping picture is Richard's comparison of the present period with the period of independence in the early nineteenth century. Since the church was divided over independence, it should not be too surprising to find that events like the Nicaraguan revolution also bring crisis and division. By the same token, both the emergence of the new society and the church's adjustment to it will undoubtedly take time.

Richard and others see this thesis on christendom as the basis for their assertion that liberation theology is not merely a left-wing version of traditional church involvement in politics. Nicaragua is a case in point. The Sandinista government does not ask the church to legitimize the revolution. The revolution is legitimized by what it does and proposes to do. Nor does the government offer any privileged place to the church. The church is free to carry out its religious mission, provided it does not seek to undermine the revolution. Church people in Nicaragua have told me they believe the bishops are uneasy in this new relationship, especially because the revolutionaries enjoy a good deal of moral leadership. The bishops interpret the end of a particular church-state alliance and their loss of a particular kind of influence in society as hostility to them and to the church.

While I find the notion of christendom helpful for looking at Latin American history, I am not altogether convinced by Richard's thesis. Seeing Nicaragua as a test case only increases my doubts.

For my part I find Joseph Comblin's treatment of christendom more persuasive. In his book *O Tempo da Ação: Ensaio Sobre o Espírito e a História* (a kind of theological reflection on various stages in church history), he does not limit himself to Latin America but examines christendom as a general phenomenon. He points out that in fact the history of christendom is not harmonious but is a history of conflict between the spiritual and temporal powers—for example, the papacy fighting for independence from the emperor. He further states that the prophetic function of the hierarchy is conceivable only within a context of christendom. That is, a prophetic voice can be heard only when there is some acknowledgment of the church's role in the public sphere.

Moreover, Comblin points out that calling for an end of christendom is nothing new. Joachim of Fiore did so in the twelfth century as did Luther and the reformers in the sixteenth century. He observes that those who set out to destroy a form of christendom usually end up building another (Calvin in Geneva, Lutheran state churches, the Puritans). In his view christendom is still strong in the United States, in a form that Robert Bellah has called "civil religion." Christendom is in decline in Western Europe, primarily because the masses themselves have lost any interest in religion, and because the state is essentially administrative and embodies no larger aim for society as a whole. In Eastern Europe communism has destroyed traditional christendom but erected in its place a counterchurch. I find his account of christendom more nuanced and more fruitful than that of Richard.

Most theological commentators evaluate christendom in entirely negative terms. Comblin acknowledges christendom's use of violence, the church's tendency to be aligned with the wealthy and to ignore evangelization, and for people to act out of conformity rather than conviction. Nevertheless, he insists that the church did not choose the alliance with civil power in christendom but was offered the opportunity. Refusal would have meant losing the opportunity to influence society as a whole. Once christendom was in place, Christians could always choose between two approaches: acting from within a position of power, or taking the side of the poor. Those who took this direction too radically, however, would find themselves condemned by society as subversive and by the church as heretical.

Although he does not expressly draw the conclusion, the upshot of Comblin's view is that it is not at all assured that what we are witnessing in Latin America is an end to christendom. In the specific case of Nicaragua, it may be that the high level of conflict there and the fact that both supporters and opponents of the revolution use religious arguments and symbols are obscuring a real move beyond christendom, as Richard argues. I tend to think, however, that if the revolution is consolidated there and if revolutions occur elsewhere in Latin America, christendom will not simply disappear but will assume another form.

9. UTILIZING MARXISM

Observations on Practice and Theology

It is not easy to have a rational discussion of Marxism in the United States. Anti-Marxism and anti-Sovietism are endemic in the United States in a way they are not in Western Europe. Many Americans are vehemently, viscerally anti-Communist, even though they have never met a living, breathing Communist. To take another example, by 1985 conventional public debate over U.S. policy toward Nicaragua was limited to whether aiding the *contras* would weaken or strengthen the Sandinistas. No member of Congress could dare say anything positive about the Nicaraguan government. That the revolutionary government in Nicaragua was Soviet-aligned and inimical to U.S. interests was taken for granted. Few noticed that such a view was not shared by virtually any other Western government, so insular was U.S. public opinion.

One of the major reasons why liberation theology is of more

than academic interest is the fact that it has some contact with Marxism. For some people that fact ends the discussion. It is my aim here to show what that contact is.

Contrary to a common stereotype, in their writings liberation theologians do not devote much space to discussing Marxism directly. Juan Luis Segundo asserts that some of the best-known theologians have only a "polite relationship" with it. Jon Sobrino comes to mind: in the eight hundred pages of his two major works, on Christ and on the church, I find nine references to Marx and none to other Marxists. In *A Theology of Liberation*, Gutiérrez refers to a wide range of Marxist literature, but there are few such references in his other works. The fundamental structure of his thought is biblical.

Yet it would be irresponsible for liberation theologians not to deal with Marxism, since it is pervasive among Latin Americans who are concerned with social change. It is as much a part of the intellectual milieu as are psychological and therapeutic concepts in the U.S. middle class. Some Latin Americans make some variety of Marxism their basic and unquestionable framework for understanding reality (as some North Americans make therapy their interpretative key). No liberation theologians are Marxists in that sense.

My aim here is not to convince anyone of the validity of Marxism but simply to show how a critical use of Marxism might make sense to Latin American theologians. First, I will look at issues arising out of the use of Marxist analysis and collaboration with Marxists, particularly in Nicaragua. I will close with some observations on points of contact between Marxist visions and liberation theology.

▪ ▪ ▪

How Marxism Is Used

For some people Marxism is a set of ready-made answers. Thus Marxist manuals tend to reduce human history to simple stages and use class struggle to provide one-dimensional explanations of complex realities. Marxist "thought" is reduced to fitting reality onto a preexisting grid.

However, Marxism can be regarded primarily as a set of questions—a method—for understanding society. At its best it can sharpen one's analysis. A friend of mine, a Nicaraguan economist, described the eye-opening effect of reading *Imperialismo y Dictadura,* an analysis of Nicaraguan economic groups by Jaime Wheelock, a Sandinista leader. "It was like seeing an X-ray of my own country," he said. My friend was certainly more highly trained than Wheelock—he had done postdoctoral work in economics at MIT. Yet Wheelock's analysis provided genuine insight.

Marxism need not be a dogmatic answers-before-the-questions ideology. It can serve heuristically to sharpen questions.

One example is the practice of "conjunctural analysis." When Latin Americans involved in pastoral work meet to plan their activities, they often begin by analyzing the *coyuntura*. The word refers to a particular moment or period—which may cover weeks, months, or even years—and especially the way the forces in society line up and interact. Typically, they will look at the actions of the armed forces, the government, business groups, political parties, labor unions, organized peasants, students, the church—in short, any organized force in society. They may also look at the international context to the extent it impinges on events. What makes such a discussion different from a bull session is the effort to make a methodical and disciplined analysis of forces at play. The aim is to situate the struggles of popular forces, and one's own pastoral efforts, within an overall context.

Such "conjunctural analysis" may have a very practical purpose—for example, to determine whether a church group should make a particular statement or carry out a particular action. There is no "right" answer; those involved must weigh the circumstances and decide how to act. What makes such "conjunctural analysis" Marxist is its systematic use of structural and class analysis.

I cite this example because the actual writings of liberation theologians often reflect a high degree of generalization. It is well to recall that they arise out of innumerable instances of analysis and action at the local level.

As I have noted, liberation theologians devote surprisingly little attention to head-on confrontation with Marxism. One exception is the 1978 document prepared by the group of theologians in Caracas, referred to in the previous chapter. In the rest of this section I will be largely restating and paraphrasing their argument while adding comments and examples for clarification.

These theologians frankly state that they do not agree with the assertion of the bishops at Medellín, who describe Latin America as "caught between" liberal capitalism and Marxism. In actuality, both capitalism and socialism assume a variety of forms. Indeed, by incorporating some elements of socialism, Western "neocapitalist societies" have largely met the basic needs of many of their citizens. That is not the case in Latin America, however.

They do not analyze the Soviet Union, but they state that "militant atheism, bureaucratism, and totalitarianism" have characterized many embodiments of Marxism, bringing on "new oppressions."

More relevant are attempts at socialism in the Third World. Without mentioning countries by name, they state that some countries "have not only met the basic needs of the majority of the people more justly, but they have achieved an independence that is national, economic, and political . . . as well as establishing forms of life and civic participation that manifest ever greater solidarity and freedom."

A comparison might illustrate what they mean. Brazil has a higher per capita income than Cuba and a far more sophisticated level of industrialization. Yet in Cuba there is none of the hunger that is widespread in Brazil. Some might grudgingly admit that perhaps there is a trade-off between satisfying people's material needs and establishing democratic freedoms. What these writers are saying, however, is that for most people in Brazil, what the dominant ideology calls freedom is an illusion. Cuba and other socialist countries, even though they do not have political parties that compete in elections, might have forms of participation that are genuine. Moreover, it may be that needed revolutionary changes can be brought about only through what some will call authoritarian rule.

In other words, rather than hold to a trade-off analysis of the relationship between basic needs and freedom, they criticize conventional notions of freedom. Elsewhere they note that some forms of "freedom" are really a "farce"; they simply cover up the freedom of a few to hold on to their wealth, derived from exploitation. They specifically mention repressive laws in Brazil and El Salvador (they are writing in 1978) as examples of how the poor majority enjoy no real freedom.

In any case, these theologians, like many other Latin Americans, are convinced that future attempts to create a new kind of society need not copy existing models, such as Cuba, but can create something new. They urge a kind of "discernment" that will lead to a "more just . . . society" with the least degree of improbability.

They make a fairly harsh judgment on many existing socialist organizations, meaning primarily, I would assume, orthodox Communist parties. They speak of their rigid orthodoxy, their messianism, their opportunism, and their infinite divisions over ideologies and programs. They see more reason for hope in newer organizations. I would assume that they had in mind the Sandinistas and other organizations developing in Central America.

They devote considerable attention to the question of "convergences" and tensions between Marxists and Christians. By "Marxists" they obviously mean people for whom Marxism supplies a basic frame of reference and may even be seen as a kind of faith. Many Christians themselves are Marxists in the more limited sense of utilizing some Marxist concepts.

There are still many resistances to such convergences on both sides. For example, some believers still hold on to the idea that Christian faith can somehow provide a world-vision or a model for how to organize society. They cannot see that a revolution must be judged on how well it meets human needs. Some Christians are afraid of being used or manipulated by Marxists, while others either fear or romanticize the masses. Revolutionary organizations, however, tend to absolutize their positions. Their theory—e.g., on the role of the proletariat—may blind them to the real people and groups in a society.

Those are just some of the resistances to a genuine collaboration between Christians and Marxists.

These theologians do not regard a future just society as a goal to be reached once and for all at a given point in time. Instead, they believe we should think of it as a "utopia and limit-concept that can arouse the best individual and collective human energies toward reaching ever closer approximations of this utopia." Those approximations, however, are "fragile and ever threatened by corruption and regression."

This striving toward utopia reveals another parallel or convergence between Marxists and Christians. On one side is an absolute humanism striving toward such a utopia through realizations that are always only relatively better than what exists and, on the other, there is a yearning for a God who is always beyond human achievements and hence demanding more. The Marxist utopia of a classless society and the Christian conviction of a transcendent God both point beyond any given human achievement.

I have been citing this analysis at some length because I believe it provides a good account of how many Christians view the "convergence" with Marxists.

Christians and Sandinistas

The kind of convergence just described became a central question with the overthrow of the Somoza dictatorship and the establishment of a revolutionary government in Nicaragua in 1979. Although the revolutionary leaders normally refer to their ideology as *sandinismo,* they do not deny that it is a kind of Marxism and even Leninism. The participation of Christians, including priests, in the government has been a point of contention since 1979.

Nicaragua may be seen as a test case for collaboration between Christians and Marxist revolutionaries. Before taking up that question, however, I will take note of the way those who oppose the Sandinistas present the revolution and the participation of Christians in it. They insist that from the very beginning the inner core of the Sandinista Front has been made up of hard-core Marxist-Leninists linked to the Soviet Union. In the late 1970s, however, the Sandinistas discovered the usefulness of linking up with middle-class and church elements. When Somoza was overthrown, they lost no time in setting about their real aim, gaining total control over Nicaragua. They have made the army and police of the nation their own army and police. They have censored the press and have used intimidation and violence against independent labor organizations and business groups. They are guilty of large-scale human rights violations, especially against the Miskito Indians. They have used intimidation and force against independent forces in the church, and at the same time they have cultivated a small group of priests and others called the "popular church," who have been very useful, particularly for deceiving international public opinion. When the pope came to Nicaragua in March 1983, Sandinista mobs insulted him. The true Catholic church is to be found in Cardinal Obando and the other bishops, the majority of the clergy and religious, and the masses of Nicaraguans, who are loyal Catholics.

I do not propose to reply point-by-point to such a litany of accusations. Rather, I would like to outline how the situation looks to those Christians who have opted to work within the revolution in Nicaragua.

First, these people believe that something new is happening in Nicaragua—for the first time Christians have participated significantly in a popular revolutionary movement not only in overthrowing the old power but in attempting to make basic changes in society.

The Sandinista National Liberation Front (FSLN) is a revolutionary organization like those that have led other historical revolutions (Russia, China, Algeria, Vietnam, Cuba, Mozambique, Angola, and so forth). Its ideology is a kind of Marxism, but it also has a strong nationalist thrust coming from the figure and ideas of Augusto César Sandino. Sandinista Marxism is not highly theoretical—one priest remarked to me that he didn't know five Nicaraguans who had read Hegel.

Although they are influenced by revolutions elsewhere, especially Cuba, the Sandinistas have not imported models. Their independence of Cuba can be seen in their approach to literacy, to health care, and particularly in their mixed economy—which is not simply a short-term tactic but a long-range recognition of economic reality—and their limited but real political pluralism.

Christians who are committed to the revolution have made that option because they believe it is the vehicle that will bring justice for the poor. The revolution in itself does not require theological justification. They do not portray it as the kingdom of God on earth but simply as a modest but real step toward a more just and more human society.

Their position is not one of uncritical support. From the beginning those Christians involved in the revolution have sought to apply the kinds of criteria outlined in the Caracas document to the situation in Nicaragua. Hence, they underline the need for austerity and for discipline, and they have warned that, like any leadership group, the FSLN runs the risk of confusing its own position with the will of the people.

In March 1981, on the first anniversary of the murder of Salvadoran Archbishop Oscar Romero, a Nicaraguan group called "Christians for the Revolution" issued a document entitled "Challenges to the Revolution." This document was at once an expression of support for the overall revolutionary process and a critique of shortcomings, such as a growing bureaucracy, a lack of austerity on the part of some leaders, mistreatment of people on the Atlantic Coast, and so forth. After two months of discussion at the local level, Christians came together for a conference at the Central American University (Jesuit) to discuss it further. Each of the seven challenges was addressed by a Christian and a representative of the FSLN. Subsequently Sandinista commanders like Tomás Borge began to incorporate some of the criticisms in their own speeches. The whole exercise was an example of what those Christian groups meant by critical support for the revolution.

Note that the so-called "popular church" in Nicaragua is not a separate organization. The term itself comes originally from Brazil (see Chapter Four) and is primarily theological. It refers to the phenomenon of the church taking root in a new way among the poor. It is associated with Christian base communities but not limited to them. In Nicaragua revolutionary Christians generally avoid the term "popular church." I believe it is especially misleading for journalists to judge the relative strength of revolutionary Christians and of those allied to the hierarchy by counting the numbers of people attending masses celebrated by Archbishop Obando and others in "revolutionary" parishes.

Since mid-1980 the Nicaraguan bishops have played an opposition role in Nicaragua. Cardinal Obando in particular is a rallying point. He frequently criticizes the government for human rights abuses, although he has never criticized the *contras,* whose pattern of terrorism against the civilian population is well documented.

The government has taken measures against church people,

sometimes expelling priests; has limited church exposure to the media; and in early 1986 closed the Catholic radio station. These actions were formally a response to violations of the law. The Sandinistas see the Catholic hierarchy as playing a major role in the U.S.-orchestrated effort to overthrow the revolution. They see their actions as legitimate reactions to the bishops' utilization of the church for manifestly political—counterrevolutionary—purposes.

Many Nicaraguan Catholics, however, support the revolution, and the relationship between Christians and the Sandinistas may be a watershed in the history of revolutions. In an October 1980 official communiqué outlining its position on religion, the FSLN stated that although some writers, reflecting the conditions of their time, have seen religion as a mechanism of alienation, that was not their experience. In other words, they were rejecting Marx's own position that religion is inevitably an opiate. In addition, they stated that no one could be excluded from the Sandinista party for religious practice. Thus, they were breaking with the official practice of all Marxist governments in power.

In this respect, Nicaragua seems to be having a significant influence on Cuba, which has followed the standard Marxist pattern of not allowing practicing believers to be members of the Communist Party. The Catholic church, for its part, long served as a refuge for those opposed to the revolution. In 1985 Fidel Castro and the Catholic bishops held their first formal meetings. The massive publication (350,000 copies) of *Fidel y la Religión*, a series of interviews between Castro and the Brazilian Dominican Frei Betto, was another sign of a major shift taking place.

▪ ▪ ▪

Dialogue with Marxist Theory

I have already noted that Latin American theologians devote surprisingly little space to a head-on discussion of Marxism. Part of the reason may be prudential, since even mentioning Marxism without clearly condemning it may invite trouble. The primary reason, I believe, it that liberation theologians accept a kind of division of labor in which their subject matter is theology, not social theory.

Nevertheless, I will close this chapter with some examples of such direct discussion.

The Mexican ex-Jesuit José Porfirio Miranda attracted considerable attention with *Marx and the Bible,* originally published in 1971. Amidst a great deal of erudition his central point is simple, namely that the core of the biblical message is that God's action (in Israel and in Jesus Christ) aims to bring about justice between human beings, and thus Marx and the Bible coincide. He further insists that since early times Christians have failed to understand this message because they have read the Bible through distorting philosophical spectacles. He stresses the moral core of Marx and finds the "gospel roots" of Marx's thought, which he regards as a "conscious continuation of early Christianity."

Others have made similar arguments, although perhaps with less intensity. Nevertheless, in positions like Miranda's I detect an implicit lack of historical sense. In other words, it seems rather essentialist to see the Scriptures as holding one—and only one—"message," that of interhuman justice and liberation. If the true meaning of that message is being uncovered only now, historical Christianity has been a two-thousand-year mistake. It seems more plausible to see the Scriptures—like any text—as open to a variety of interpretations, some of which will be developed only when human society has reached certain conditions. The Apostle Paul, for example, spoke of Christianity as doing away with distinctions between slave and free, male and female. Yet he did not critique slavery as an institution, and his thought is full of patriarchal imagery and assumptions. Until recent centuries it was impossible to conceive of conscious human activity to modify or even overthrow institutions in society. A liberating reading of the Scripture not only can but must be different from a first-century reading.

To move to a different kind of contact with Marxism, intuitively some theologians and pastoral workers have seen existing society as practicing idolatry, since the wealth of a few prevails over the life of human beings. Franz Hinkelammert, a German who has worked for twenty years in Latin America, and the Brazilian Hugo Assmann have turned to Marx's concept of fetishism to flesh out this idea.

Hinkelammert follows Marx's analysis of fetishism in *Capital.* Human beings at first produced "use-values" for their own subsistence, for example, a crop to eat. However, at a given point they began to produce goods for their "exchange-value." At that point fetishism begins: human beings are dominated by the commodities they produce. Commodities become "subjects" acting apparently by themselves (e.g., coffee "dancing" on world markets) while living human beings become objects. Those who produce commodities—the workers—are prevented from organizing how they will be divided and distributed. Matters only become worse, with "money fetishism" and "capital fetishism." Hinkelammert's *The Ideological Weapons of Death* is a fierce critique of fetishism in thinkers like Max Weber, Milton Friedman, and Karl Popper.

Assmann and Hinkelammert both emphasize that Marx's analysis of fetishism uses religious images. Thus, money itself is frequently a "god" or divinity or an idol or Mammon. Marx sees capital as Moloch, the idol who demands human sacrifice.

Assmann strongly argues that these are not simple literary figures and that fetishism is an essential category for understanding capitalism. The world turns topsy-turvy and reality becomes obscured. People cannot see the essence of social phenomena but only their appearance.

> Things move persons, since fetishism has changed things into subjects and subjects into things. Marx calls this basic characteristic of capitalism the "religious quid pro quo." . . . By fetishizing reality, the capitalist system is by its very nature idolatrous.

Revolutions are necessarily "atheistic," since they amount to an apostasy from the enthroned idols which are overthrown. Assmann concludes that "just as there is no faith in the God of Life without putting aside the idols that kill, neither is there social revolution without putting aside the fetishes that legitimize and hold oppression together; that is, there is no revolution without 'faith' in the struggle for life and without organizing people's hope."

Assmann and Hinkelammert believe that fetishism is central to Marx's critique of capitalism and that the presence of religious images is not accidental. They see this critique as an essential tool for unmasking idols today.

10. GOD OF LIFE

The Religious Vision of Liberation Theology

AT THE CORE OF LIBERATION THEOLOGY IS A SPIRITUALITY, a religious vision. It is an experience of God within the suffering and struggle of the poor. The written theology produced is an attempt to explicate—and sometimes to defend—that religious experience and vision.

This exposition began with the "option for the poor" and some description of the kind of biblical reading that takes place in Christian base communities. More recent chapters have focused more on ideological and institutional questions. Even the most apparently arcane questions are related to the poor and their struggle for a more just society. Poor Latin Americans may not understand an analysis of Marx's treatment of fetishism in *Capital,* but they can understand a God of life and they can understand how forces of death are embodied in seemingly sacred realities like private property.

I will here be considering some of the central theological preoccupations in Latin America. Some of these themes have been touched on earlier, particularly in Chapter Three.

God of Life and Idols of Death

Theology is theo-logy: talk about God. I recall being struck by a remark of Jon Sobrino in El Salvador. He said that many theologians seemed to be writing about theology—hence the many references to other theologians—rather than about God. The next time I picked up one of his writings I was struck by the directness and immediacy with which he spoke of God.

In North America and Europe the "God problem" is essentially one of how one can believe in God at all. Certainly, many people still find comfort and meaning in traditional forms of Christianity, such as the estimated thirty million or more fundamentalists in the United States. They seem to have no "God problem." But for many people traditional belief seems highly problematic. Isn't Christianity simply one of many human projections? How can anyone believe in a God who can tolerate Nazi death camps? What difference does it make whether one believes or not? Even theologians themselves ask these questions in Europe and North America.

The situation in Latin America is quite different. In the first place, unbelief is not a widespread pastoral problem except among small elites. Ordinary people, the poor, continue to believe in a more or less traditional manner. That situation, of course, could change. Religion, and specifically Roman Catholicism, has a larger public role in Latin America than it does in Europe or even the United States, where religion's role is more diffused. During the 1970s military dictators were eager to take part in public acts such as dedicating their country to the Sacred Heart or to the Virgin Mary. At the extreme, people can be tortured and murdered in the name of the Christian God. Hence, in a pastoral and theological sense the "God question" becomes not whether there exists some referent to the term "God" but which God is meant.

Here the theologians have retrieved an ancient biblical theme, that of "idolatry." Many passages in the Hebrew Bible are polemics against the gods of neighboring peoples. The Mosaic God contrasts sharply with those other gods, some of which even demand human sacrifice. He is associated with acts of liberation: the exodus from Egypt and the arrival in a new land. Biblical scholars draw the contrast with the traits of the neighboring gods. They are cosmic divinities while he is a Lord of human history. They are tied to the royal courts, with their priesthoods, armies, and tribute systems, while the Hebrew God is associated with a group of slaves, who later live as a confederation of tribes. They demand elaborate rituals, while he demands justice and fair conduct.

That is something of an ideal type, however, for in practice Hebrew society took on some of the characteristics of neighboring peoples. With Saul, David, and Solomon Israel became a monarchy. In theory, the king was to protect the poor; in practice, however, Israel had a royal court, a priesthood, and armies, and it alternately went to war and made alliances with neighboring kingdoms. It is Israel's failure to live up to its original calling that prompts the rise of prophecy.

Biblical religion in general is a reaction against the mythological view, which sees things as they are now, both in the cosmos and in human culture, as given and as part of an overarching divine order. Being tied to an "eternal return" symbolized in the seasons, worship reinforces an image of all reality as fixed. The biblical pattern, by contrast, is historical: Israel's relationship with Yahweh is the result of a series of acts of liberation. A basic metaphor is that of a journey—an exodus—toward a future point. Human culture is dedivinized, and decosmicized, thus freeing people to work out their own future, always in accord with God's aim. In the New Testament idolatry refers not so much to religious practices as to the pursuit of money, power, or pleasure.

Latin American theologians have dusted off the category of idolatry and made it central to their theology as an ever present tendency. At Puebla the bishops say people fall into slavery "when they divinize or absolutize wealth, power, the State, sex, pleasure, or anything created by God—including their own being or human reason. God himself is the source of radical liberation from all forms of idolatry. . . ." The bishops quote Jesus: "You cannot give yourself to God and money" (Luke 16:13). Political power can also be divinized when it becomes an absolute. Totalitarian use of power "is a form of idolatry." Like the ancient gods, such as Moloch, who demanded sacrifices, sometimes of human beings, modern idols also demand life.

Idolatry is not simply an Old Testament theme. Examining the gospel accounts, Jon Sobrino finds that Jesus reveals and defends a "God of life" and engages in struggle with false divinities. Jesus' message that it is the poor and the outcast who are invited to the kingdom and his actions of welcoming the sick, tax collectors, and prostitutes arouse controversy and opposition. Jesus has harsh criticism for the elites: the rich, the priests, Pharisees, scribes, and rulers. Generalizing on the particular cases, Sobrino asserts that in the controversies, and behind disputes about the law, is a conflict between a God of life, and divinities that bring death. "The sabbath was made for human beings, not human beings for the sabbath." Jesus unmasks the use of the symbol of God to put others to death, and that is why he is himself killed.

Jesus is not simply defending one set of ideas about God over against another but is defending the God of life. Sobrino does not explicitly draw the conclusion, but it is clear that something similar can still happen, that is, that some can invoke the Christian God in order to take the life of other human beings. In such a case a struggle for the true God of life will not only be justified but even necessary.

At one point Sobrino quotes the saying of Saint Irenaeus (d. c. 200): *"Gloria Dei, vivens homo"*—"God's glory is the living human being." Archbishop Romero commented on this slogan more than once, probably borrowing it from Sobrino, who was working in El Salvador. On the other hand, Sobrino's perception of a conflict between a God of life and divinities of death in the gospel was undoubtedly stimulated by the struggle of Romero and others on behalf of peasants, and the assurance with which the powerful used violence to defend "Christian" civilization.

Sobrino goes on to put a twist on the traditional concept of God's transcendence. Ordinarily, transcendence, God's "beyondness," is contrasted with immanence, God's presence "within" human and earthly experience and reality. A common approach is to try to "balance" both aspects. Liberation theology is sometimes accused of ignoring transcendence, of falling into "horizontalism"—that is, of being too concerned about the earthly and of lacking a sufficient "vertical" dimension.

Sobrino is in effect recasting the discussion—indeed, claiming that Jesus has recasted it. God's preferential love for the poor introduces a tension within human history between what is and what should be. "And the history that is generated when one attempts to live according to God's love transcends itself, and is therefore a mediation of God's transcendence." In accordance with the traditional notion, Sobrino says God is always greater than any human realization or even any human ability to conceive. But far from that being a motive for quietism (if God is utterly "beyond," why bother to act within human history, since it is ultimately insignificant?) it should be a pull toward making love effective within human history.

Sobrino and other theologians have sought to present a pastorally appropriate Christology. In traditional churches one can find gory statues and paintings of a suffering Jesus but few of Christ in glory. People organize great pageants reenacting Good Friday, or processions with participants dressed in penitential purple or carrying heavy images of saints. Yet Holy Week seems to end there, with Jesus on the cross. Poor people find a real consolation in knowing that Jesus suffered before them. In seeking to explain the meaning of Jesus' death "for our sins," traditional Catholic theology seemed to hold that the crucifixion was the price that God demanded for sin.

In reaction there can be a facile emphasis on the resurrection, or sometimes on the whole cycle of incarnation-death-resurrection that takes the bite out of Jesus' death. Latin American theologians have not looked for a superficial "balance" but rather have sought to see the connections between the way Jesus lived, his death, and the resurrection.

Jesus' death is the direct outgrowth of his life and mission. It was his preaching and action that created those enemies who eventually determined to have him killed. His preaching was a radical critique of those who held power. It was not a revolutionary call to organized resistance, for example, like that of the Zealots, a sect that struggled for independence from Roman domination. Liberation theologians have not tried to recast Jesus as a social revolutionary. Such an attempt would be unhistorical and indeed anachronistic. Jesus' message, however, contains the seeds of a critique of any use of power that would bring death to human beings.

Jesus' death was something real in history, the product of his own human decision and the decisions of others. He was not simply acting out a prewritten script, as some traditional notions might lead one to believe.

His suffering was compounded by a genuine agony of abandonment, not only by his disciples but even by God his Father. Not only was he being killed, but it seemed as though the kingdom he preached would not be achieved. His response was to maintain fidelity to the end.

On the cross God takes on human suffering, becomes himself a "crucified God". The cross breaks any easy ideas of God. It reveals the deepest meaning of human suffering, particularly the unjust suffering of the poor.

The resurrection is God's vindication of Jesus and his message and is the basis for a new life of faith. The God of life triumphs over the forces—the gods—of death. Morever, in the resurrection the real human history of Jesus' life and death sets in motion further history as people seek to live out the new life.

The preceding paragraphs are a condensed version of major Christological themes in Latin America. Many people, ordinary poor people, have taken this image of Jesus to heart. They are at home with his words in Scripture, and they see this pattern of life-death-resurrection as a pattern for their own life. They point to small achievements in their own community as examples of the kingdom, or as a new life of resurrection. Jesus' own life—historical in his time—becomes historical in them.

Latin American theology tends to be very Christological, very Christ-focused, starting with the humanity of Jesus of Nazareth. This is a reaction against an earlier focus on God, conceived in largely metaphysical terms, and on Jesus as "both God and man," very removed from normal human experience.

Such a focus could lead to one-sidedness, to what some have called "Christo-monism," whose effects can be seen in the history of the church and throughout Western history and culture. For example, the Catholic church's imperial style is justified by the notion that it is the "continuation of Christ incarnate in the world." An adequate theology of the Holy Spirit would point in a different direction. Comblin has written extensively on the need to understand the mission of the Holy Spirit, a spirit of newness and diversity in history.

Kingdom and Church

Liberation theology articulates an experience of God in the poor that takes place in the church. From the outset it has been strongly "ecclesial" (from Greek *ekklēsia*)—that is, it has had a strong focus on the church.

"The church is not the kingdom; it is to serve the kingdom."

That dictum is a kind of first principle of Latin American ecclesiology. The gospels show Jesus preaching not himself but his Father's kingdom. Over the centuries, however, the church has often preached itself as the depository of God's grace and truth, entrusted to it by Jesus. The image of Jesus as a heavenly monarch—an image reinforced by hierarchs in courtly garments—was part of the same conviction.

Today theologians for the most part do not see Jesus as having "founded" the church by commissioning Peter with the keys of the kingdom. Whatever may have been Jesus' awareness when he died—and it is quite possible that, seeing the apparent failure of his mission, he could only trust in God—the church itself grew out of a "Jesus movement" that sprang up in the wake of his resurrection. The Scriptures are the recollection of his followers during the early decades.

Vatican II spoke of the church serving "the world." The Latin American emphasis, that it is to serve the kingdom, gives some sense of what that service is to be. The kingdom is a situation in which people can live together as brothers and sisters. As such it is a utopia, but a utopia that impels people to work here and now for "partial realizations" of that kingdom. Thus, Nicaraguan Christians who are committed to the revolution do not believe that it—or any form of organization in society—will be the kingdom. Nevertheless, they believe that it does indeed offer the possibility of a more real kind of solidarity among people and is thereby a modest but real "approximation" of the kingdom.

The practical pastoral implication is that the church finds its raison d'être not in itself but in the community it is to serve. For the larger church institution this means that its criterion should not simply be how well it is faring institutionally. Again, to take the Nicaraguan case, its criterion should not be how well Catholic schools are doing, or how much prestige or power the church as an institution enjoys under the revolution, but what serves the kingdom. Similarly, at the barrio or village level the concern of the base community should not be primarily how to attract more members but how to serve the whole community. This is not an idle point, since such groups, like sects, have a temptation to take an in-group/out-group attitude and even a moralizing tone toward those who do not join or who perhaps "fall away."

The Caracas theologians already mentioned express this point in different language. They say that what is most important is the "primary ecclesiality," which they define as "the real life of Christian men and women who know that they make up a people and stand in solidarity, people who have a mission in and for Latin America, and who have found their ultimate identity by becoming a church of the poor." Out of this comes a "secondary ecclesiality," namely an "organic configuring of the church of the poor into structures that are doctrinal, sacramental, administrative, and hierarchical."

They do not advocate some kind of non- or anti-institutional church, or some rebel or parallel church. Experience has shown that structures are necessary. What they insist on is that church structures and procedures, even sacraments and worship, take their significance from the primary experience of God among the poor, and not the other way around.

The two major images of the church to come out of Vatican II were those of "people of God" and "sacrament." "People of God" is of course the biblical image of the Hebrew people in exodus. With the notion of a journey—that is, something unfinished and open, it was clearly a corrective to the Roman Catholic pretension to be the possessor of truth and grace. Its egalitarian thrust was also a corrective to the pyramidal notion of authority in which those above—pope, bishops, priests—are somehow "more" church than ordinary believers. What Latin American theology has added is the notion of *el pueblo de los pobres*—the people of the poor. *Pueblo* is really untranslatable: literally, it means "the people," but it also means the mass of the people—poor people in contrast to the elites. If the church is to be the "people of God," it is not in an undifferentiated sense but as the people of the poor with whom God stands in solidarity.

"Sacrament" means both "mystery" and "sign." Vatican II's

now classic formulation is that by its relationship with Christ, the church is "a kind of sacrament or sign of intimate union with God, and of the unity of all humankind." Again, the implication is that the church does not exist for itself alone but for all of humankind. Its function is to be a kind of sign of God's presence and design for humanity. Latin American theologians have further specified that the church is called to be a sign of liberation in history.

Elsewhere I have described some of the activities of the church in Latin America. In addition to pastoral work in small communities, the church has used its institutional resources to aid and defend victims of repression, has documented and denounced human rights abuses, and has publicly criticized development models. Jon Sobrino asks how the various services the church provides should be understood, what they have in common. He answers that it is "witness on behalf of life." Christians are to bear witness to the mediation of God in Jesus, not in some compartmentalized religious sphere but in life as a whole. That entails struggle against injustice. "Witness to God the creator necessarily becomes witness to God the liberator." This is all the more true insofar as the "reigning structures—capitalism and national security in their many forms—operate as true deities with divine characteristics and their own cult. They are deities because they claim characteristics that belong to God also: ultimateness, definitiveness, and untouchability. They have their own cult because they demand the daily sacrificing of the majority and the violent sacrificing of those who oppose them."

In this context the service of the church consists of "the ongoing humanization of the human realm at every level and in every situation."

Some of these general ideas on the church come together in the experience of the Eucharist. Communion is celebrated both by a small circle of people from the base community and in larger gatherings. Outwardly, it may seem humble indeed: peasants, perhaps barefoot, people who by themselves have no power in society. Together they repeat the action of Jesus, and he is present in their midst in a meal. That meal is both what Jesus commanded—"Do this in memory of me"—and a token of what God promises, a wedding feast for all. They listen to the Scriptures and see their own experience reflected there.

An example of how important the Eucharist is for some people comes from Guatemala. In mid-1980, after two priests had been murdered and the bishop had escaped an ambush, all the priests and sisters left the diocese of Quiché. Army repression increased to the point where mass killings became routine. During this time catechists traveled many miles through mountains to neighboring dioceses to receive consecrated bread and carry it back hidden perhaps in tortillas for communion in their villages.

That communion was a sign of hope and resurrection, helping them to resist and struggle for a fuller life.

11. OTHER ACCENTS

Third World, Black, Hispanic, and Feminist Theologies

LATIN AMERICAN LIBERATION THEOLOGY IS NOT AN ISOLATED phenomenon. Parallel theologies—Asian, African, black, and feminist—have arisen out of struggles. All represent reactions against a European and North American theological establishment that unconsciously assumed that its theology was simply "Christian" theology. Each of these new theologies has become critical of the inherited way of interpreting Christian symbols. Feminist theologians have extended their critique to the symbols themselves and question the "maleness" of the deity, for example. Each has reinterpreted the past to find its own history, which has been largely suppressed from memory by the dominant interpretations.

Dialogue between these new theologies became formalized in the Theology in the Americas conferences held in Detroit in 1975 and 1980 and at conferences at several sites from 1976 onward under the auspices of the Ecumenical Association of Third World Theologians. But dialogue has not always been easy. To black theologians Latin Americans seemed to want to impose a narrowly economic interpretation of oppression and to be insufficiently sensitive to racism; Latin Americans, for their part, believed black theologians did not have a sufficiently systemic understanding of oppression. Feminists saw both Latin American and black theology as mainly male enterprises, even though the theologians, sensitized by contact with feminism occasionally mentioned the oppression of women. Although participants in the dialogue could agree that imperialism, classism, racism, and sexism are "interstructured" and reinforce one another and that a dominant form of civilization run by and for the benefit of white Western males is at the root of oppression, there was no easy synthesis.

The various liberation theologies agree that a major development is that those who have been overlooked and excluded—the poor, nonwhites, women—are breaking into history. At the 1981 conference in New Delhi the dominant theme became the "irruption" of the excluded, an

> irruption of exploited classes, marginalized cultures and humiliated races. They are bursting from the underside of history into the world long dominated by the West. It is an irruption expressed in revolutionary struggles, political uprisings, and liberation movements. It is an irruption of religious and ethnic groups looking for affirmation of their authentic identity, of women demanding recognition and equality, of youth protesting dominant systems and values. It is an irruption of all those who struggle for full humanity and for their rightful place in history.

In what follows I will show some points of contact between Latin American theology and other forms of liberation theology.

▪ ▪ ▪

Asian and African Theology

The Christian churches in Asia and Africa share certain characteristics that set them apart from Latin American Christianity. They are largely the product of the missionary expansion of European churches during the nineteenth and twentieth centuries, while Latin American Catholicism arrived as part of sixteenth-century Iberian expansion. Catholicism has a cultural quasi-monopoly in Latin America, while in Asia and Africa (with the exception of the Philippines) Christians are a small and often tiny minority.

Christians in Asia confront a vast variety of socioeconomic and historical contexts, from giant India to a city-state like Hong Kong, and religious contexts varying from pluralism of India to Indonesia, which is 90 percent Muslim. Christians from the People's Republic of China have not been involved in the dialogue, but ultimately China cannot be ignored in any Asian dialogue. Christians in Africa also confront widespread diversity, from the apartheid regime in South Africa, to the experiment with *ujamaa* socialism in Tanzania, to oil-producing Nigeria, and so forth.

For some time it has been obvious that the missionaries brought *Western* Christianity and that a major task is to develop suitable Asian and African forms of worship and theology. This effort antedates liberation theology. African theologians speak of coming to a fuller comprehension of "African anthropology," their continent's particular sense of the human being and the cosmos. Asian theology involves encounters with Buddhism, Hinduism, Islam, and other traditions in their many historic forms.

These efforts are often referred to by the shorthand phrase "inculturation" to indicate that the imported Western Christian churches must find ways of incorporating Asian and African cultures and of being incorporated into them. Insofar as this amounts to affirming their own being as Asians and Africans, the inculturation movement can be regarded as liberating.

Some movements parallel Latin American liberation theology even more closely. A clear instance is the participation of Christians in the struggle against the apartheid regime in South Africa. In 1985 a group of church people produced a manifesto called the "Kairos document" that explicitly criticized the "state theology" used to justify the regime and the "church theology" that impeded involvement out of a fear of involvement in politics. Many Filipino church people struggled against the Marcos dictatorship out of a kind of liberation theology, although there does not seem to be much published theology.

During the 1960s theologians in Korea developed *minjung* theology. The term *minjung* defies definition, but one attempt is that it designates "a people politically oppressed, economically poor, and socially and culturally alienated, yet seeking to be the artisan of its own destiny in an active way." This *minjung* theology has developed out of the experience and struggles of Christians with the poor. Some find this approach too narrow and insist that the central problem of Korea is its division into south and north, a division which the anticommunism of the churches has fostered. Hence, they call for a critique of this Christian anticommunism, "not in the light of communism but in the light of biblical faith in God's justice for the world."

Sri Lankan Catholic theologian Tissa Balasuriya's book *Planetary Theology* offers an Asian liberation theology. Yet there is an undeniable tension between inculturationist and liberationist approaches in Africa and Asia. Another Sri Lankan, Aloysius Pieris, is convinced that the inculturationist/liberationist dichotomy is false. He says that Asian cultures, popular as well as high, put people in contact with the basic truths of every religion, each in a new way: "the meaning and destiny of human existence; crippling human limitations and our infinite capacity to break through them; liberation both human and cosmic; in short, *the struggle for a full humanity*." He says that every Asian culture is built up around a "soteriological nucleus" ("soteriology" means "doctrine of salvation"). "The Asian theology of liberation lies hidden there, waiting to be discovered by whoever is ready to 'sell all things.' "

Pieris points to cosmic and metacosmic elements in Asian religiosity. The foundation of this religiosity is cosmic religion, which is sometimes pejoratively called "animism" when in reality it is the posture of all human beings toward natural forces. In Africa and Oceania cosmic religion can appear in its pure form; in Asia however, metacosmic soteriologies—Hinduism, Buddhism, and Taoism to some extent—have been built over it. These soteriologies produce spiritual elites—monks—who serve as models of liberated existence. Mutuality between the cosmic and metacosmic levels is exemplified by the relationship between the Buddhist monastic community and the rest of society. This relationship appears in the bipolarity between wealth and poverty, the state and the *sangha* (the monastic community), and scientific knowledge and spiritual wisdom. In Asia, says Pieris, the antonym to poverty is not wealth but "acquisitiveness." "The primary concern, therefore, is not the elimination of poverty but struggle against Mammon."

Asian Christian churches are caught between classical theology and liberation theology, both Western. Nevertheless, in liberation theology's method Pieris sees the direction the Asian churches should take. He stresses the "primacy of praxis over theory" and insists on the importance of finding God in poverty. At the same time, he accepts "the liberation theologian's option for socialism, i.e., for a definite social order in which oppressive structures are changed radically, even violently, in order to allow every person to be fully human, the assumption being that no one is liberated unless everyone is."

In examining the approaches of the churches to Asia, Pieris distinguishes two alternating approaches, which he calls "Christ-against-religions" and "Christ-of-religions." Christ can be regarded as standing against "false" religions or indeed against all religions when Christianity itself is seen as not being a religion (Karl Barth). Pieris points out that some Latin American theologians—Miranda and even Sobrino—reflect this Western and colonialist approach. Although he is more sympathetic to the

"Christ-of-religion" tendency, which sees Jesus Christ as the fulfillment of religious striving, Pieris points out how it has tended to ignore the role of religion in structural poverty and struggles for liberation.

From an Asian viewpoint "religion is life itself rather than a function of it, being the all-pervasive ethos of human existence." It is the West that has had a narrow definition of religion. "A true revolution cannot go against religion in its totality. If a revolution succeeds, it does so normally as a cathartic renewal of religion itself." "No *true* liberation is possible unless persons are 'religiously motivated' toward it."

Contrary to stereotypes about non-Christian religions being "world-denying," Pieris insists on their liberatory thrust. These religions do not envision the ultimate reality as a "personal being" and indeed are metatheistic, or at least nontheistic. Hence the starting point for collaboration is not "God-talk" (theology) but liberation. He proposes that "the religious instinct be defined as a revolutionary urge, a psycho-social impulse, to generate a new humanity." He integrates revolution and religion into a framework in which the process of humanization is part of the evolution of the cosmos itself.

Pieris may not be typical of Asian theologians, but the sweep of his ideas gives a hint of how the dialogue between continents may develop.

Black Theology

Black theology in the United States, the Caribbean, and Africa parallels Latin American theology in numerous ways. Its exponents also broke away from the theology they had learned in seminaries and yet remained in dialogue with it. As Latin American theology reflected a move from developmentalism to liberation, black theology reflected the passage from the ideal of integration to that of black power. After a period of manifestos and first maps of the new theology, black theologians took a new look at their history in order to retrieve their past. They have also sought to relate to the faith of people in the black churches, just as Latin Americans entered into contact with popular Catholicism. In reading the Scriptures out of the black experience, black theologians use the basic paradigm of "liberation" and often focus on the same texts and motifs used in Latin America, especially the exodus and the figure of Jesus. James Cone's polemic assertion that "Christ is black," which many whites found offensive, is similar to the Latin American conviction that God takes sides with the poor.

The first expressions of black theology can be traced to events within black church structures in the mid-1960s. Black ministers found themselves caught between events in the black community and the structures and procedures of the churches. Inspired by Malcom X, newer leaders like Stokely Carmichael were calling for black power, as opposed to the integration that Martin Luther King and others had assumed to be the goal of the struggle. Younger blacks were either leaving the churches or joining the Nation of Islam, thus rejecting a Christianity assumed to be part of the white power structure.

Black church leaders faced a pastoral dilemma. They did not want to go against Martin Luther King. Moreover, whites, and some blacks, were made uneasy by the cry for black power, which seemed to suggest violence. Some whites who felt they had been allies in the civil rights struggle now felt snubbed. There were warnings that black power could endanger the "gains" made in civil rights. Addressing some of these anxieties, in July 1966 the National Committee of Negro Churchmen issued a statement endorsing the concept of black power. They noted that the historical experience of forming their own black churches—after being forced out of white churches—had in fact given "Negroes" a degree of power. On the other hand, they admitted that the Negro church had often presented an "*otherworldly* conception of God's power."

That statement would look mild only three years later. In

May 1969 James Forman presented to the Riverside Church of New York City a document adopted at the National Black Economic Development Conference, held a few days earlier in Detroit. The core of the document was a demand that "the white Christian churches and Jewish synagogues, which are part and parcel of the system of capitalism . . . begin to pay reparations to black people in this country." The amount was set at $500 million: "This total comes to fifteen dollars per nigger." If this demand, described as modest, was not met, they threatened that churches and church institutions would be disrupted.

It was in this context of radicalization that the term "black theology" began to appear. In 1969 James Cone published *Black Theology and Black Power,* and the term was soon reflected in numerous conferences and articles. The National Committee of Black Churchmen produced a statement on black theology calling it

> a theology of black liberation . . . a theology of "blackness." It is the affirmation of black humanity that emancipates black people from white racism, thus providing authentic freedom for both white and black people. . . .
>
> The message of liberation is the revelation of God as revealed in the incarnation of Jesus Christ. Freedom IS the gospel. Jesus is the Liberator! The demand that Christ the Liberator imposes on all men *requires* all blacks to affirm their full dignity as persons and all whites to surrender their presumptions of superiority and abuses of power.

Black theologians, at least as I read them, tend to center on scriptural motifs very similar to those used by Latin American theologians. Naturally, they are most concerned about racism: the history of slavery, racism as systemic and institutionalized, and its cultural impact. They reject theories that simply subsume racism into an overarching scheme; hence, they are suspicious of Marxism. Nevertheless, theologians like James Cone have entered into serious dialogue with Marxism, a dialogue which has gone furthest perhaps with Cornel West.

Hispanic Theology

The first expressions of an emerging Hispanic consciousness in the church in the United States did not take the form of theology but rather of a demand for recognition within the Catholic church. There are fifteen million or more Hispanics in the United States. Most are Catholics, although Protestant churches, especially of the pentecostal variety, are growing rapidly. Despite the fact that approximately one-third of all U.S. Catholics are Hispanics or of Hispanic origins, the Catholic church has been slow to recognize the implications of this fact.

In the late 1960s a priests' group called Padres began organizing so that Hispanics would have a rightful place in the church, as did a similar group of nuns called Hermanas. One of the demands of Padres was that more Hispanic bishops be appointed, and that began to happen during the mid-1970s. The deeper concern of these groups, however, was to find an appropriate form of pastoral work with Hispanics. Virgilio Elizondo and others set up the Mexican American Cultural Center (MACC) in San Antonio as a training center for nuns, priests, and lay pastoral workers. Latin American theologians like Enrique Dussel were among the invited professors.

There was no automatic or easy way to apply Latin American theology and pastoral methods to Hispanics in the United States. The history, culture, experience, and mind-set of the different groups vary greatly: from the immigrants from Mexico (and Central America) in the Southwest, to Puerto Ricans in New York, to largely middle-class Cubans in Florida. All are torn between their culture and the pressures of "making it" in the United States. Frequently, there is an observable progression from a Spanish-speaking immigrant generation, to a bilingual second generation, to a third generation speaking only English. Hence, there is no easy transplant of Latin American theology.

There is nevertheless a good deal of pastoral renewal. Some parishes have put into operation adaptations of a base-community pastoral strategy. One expression of this vitality has been the organization of *Encuentros* (*encuentro* means "encounter, meeting, conference") in 1972, 1977, and 1985. The *Encuentros* have been a process of consultation, beginning at the parish level and then moving to the diocesan level, with courses, discussions, and meetings. Regional- and national-level conferences have thus provided a kind of forum in which Hispanic Catholics could express what they wanted to see in the church.

Possibly reflecting their contact with Latin American theologians, those active in this pastoral renewal have used phrases like "liberation" and *concientización*. Nevertheless, I find that although they occasionally make passing references to a larger systemic critique of the economic system, their primary concern is to assert their own cultural identity. In this they may faithfully reflect the Hispanic communities, in which only a small proportion arrives at a radical critique. This is clearest in the case of the Cuban community, for whom the United States represented deliverance from a Marxist revolution, but it is also largely true of those whose origins are in Mexico, Puerto Rico, or elsewhere.

To my knowledge, there is only one book-length expression of a Hispanic theology, Virgilio Elizondo's *Galilean Journey: The Mexican-American Promise*. The title comes from the polarity between Galilee and Jerusalem found in the gospels. Jesus is from Galilee, a region that the "purer" Jews of Jerusalem regard with disdain. One reason for this disdain was the fact that the Galileans were of mixed blood. They were the result of a *mestizaje*—like Mexican-Americans. It was in this place far from the centers of power that Jesus carried out his ministry among the poor and the outcast. In the end, he went to Jerusalem to confront those centers of power and was killed.

This polarity provides Elizondo with a basic paradigm for his own exploration of the historical and cultural experience of Mexican-American *mestizaje*. Like Enrique Dussel, Elizondo begins the story with the conquest of 1492, and like liberation theologians he finds resonances between the biblical experience and that of Mexican-Americans. He focuses on the figure of Jesus and does not make the exodus a major symbol. Elizondo explicitly states that Mexican-Americans must face up to "racism and liberal capitalism," although he is equally explicit in stating that to embrace Marxism would be "to trade one form of enslavement for another." Elizondo's primary concern is to carry out a theological exploration—and validation—of Mexican-American culture rather than a systemic critique of the dominant U.S. society. In this he reflects the prevailing tendency in pastoral renewal among Hispanics.

Feminist Liberation Theology

A new feminist theology has arisen parallel to other liberation theologies since the 1960s. Like them it is a theological reflection of a liberation movement in the society as a whole. Part of the initial work has been a retrieval of the past, seeking elements in the history of Christianity that had been ignored or suppressed by male-dominated theology. Feminist theology assumes a new method, a new way of doing theology.

Latin American theology has been mainly a male enterprise, male in its personnel—virtually all the well-known theologians are men—and in its viewpoint and methods. Since the mid-1970s Latin American theologians have been somewhat sensitized to the more overt manifestations of sexism. Women like Beatriz Couch (Argentina), Julia Esquivel (Guatemala), and Elsa Tamez (Costa Rica) participate in theological meetings and projects. In their analyses of the "Latin American reality" Latin Americans now incorporate references to women as being doubly exploited (or triply if they are Indians or blacks). They stress the positive role of women in the struggle for justice and the contribution women already make to pastoral work in the church, with a recognition that they are underrepresented in leadership roles with power.

The feminist dimension brings up an undeniable tension in Latin American theology. Latin American feminists, including theologians, do not wish to import North American and European feminism. They are careful to place the women's agenda within an overall liberation context rather than have it compete with economic and political liberation. They envision a liberation that will enable women to participate on a footing of equality in building a new kind of society. They do not advocate a strategy of pitting women against men in any way that would weaken the overall liberation struggle. Nevertheless, there is a strong tendency for males to dismiss feminism as a bourgeois import and to simply tuck women's rights into an agenda to be dealt with in the future.

For the most part, Latin American liberation theologians, while they are quite willing to consider the more obvious demands for equality between men and women and to work against the more obvious manifestations of sexism, have yet to come to grips with the more radical implications of feminist thinking, and feminist theology in particular. That seems to be true even of feminist theologians in Latin America, at least as expressed in a conference entitled "The Latin American Woman: the Praxis and Theology of Liberation" held in Mexico City in October 1979.

The participants in that seminar were not primarily professional theologians but those working with poor women. In their final document they list the particular characteristics of the double exploitation of poor women in Latin America as well as its justification in macho ideology. The church is said to be a "patriarchal structure." They note that, despite the prominent place of women in Christian communities, theology does not take women sufficiently into account. If the "people's church" is to make progress and if liberation theology is to mature, the issue of the situation of women must be part of all theological endeavor. They urge that women be allowed to specialize in theology and take their place as organic intellectuals in the struggle for change.

In their actual reading of the Scriptures, however, they look mainly for biblical motifs supporting male-female equality. They note that "church tradition has injected antifemale prejudices" in its reading of the Bible but do not raise the possibility that those texts themselves reflect considerable patriarchy. In a word, it seems to me that Latin American theology is willing to deal with sexism to some extent but has yet to incorporate the critique of patriarchy.

Feminism is sometimes taken to be simply a fight for women's rights, for equal treatment, and, in fact, much of the day-to-day business of the women's movement can be seen that way—e.g., the struggle for the ERA or the struggle for equality in pay. In the churches the struggle for the ordination of women could be seen to be analogous.

However, if the evil is not just "sexism"—unequal treatment—but patriarchy, a profound evil going back to the roots of civilization and running through all recorded history, complete solutions will not be found even in a socialist revolution. From this angle the implications of feminist theology are more radical than those of Latin American theology.

This difference is manifest in their differing approaches to Scripture. Latin American theology accepts the findings of biblical scholarship about the original meaning of the texts as elaborated in the course of Hebrew history and in early Christian communities. It parts company with most European biblical scholarship in its *hermeneutics,* that is, in the way it interprets the meaning of these texts today. However, the original meaning in itself is not seen as problematic.

Feminist scholarship, however, is willing to question that original sense. The place of women in early Christian communities furnishes an example. At first glance, nothing is more obvious than male dominance: all the apostles are men, most of the people with active roles are men, and women say relatively little. However, applying scholarly suspicion, Elizabeth

Schüssler-Fiorenza and Luise Schottroff find evidence that women in the early communities played an active role as "apostles, missionaries, patrons, co-workers, prophets, and leaders of communities"—this even in the Pauline writings. An important figure is Mary of Magdala (Magdalene), who is one of the first witnesses of the resurrection. The Scriptures reflect some rivalry on the part of Peter.

How explain, then, the texts in which Paul admonishes women to keep their head covered, and in general keep their place? They point to a process of "patriarchalization" in which the immediate liberating impulse of the Jesus movement was tamed under pressure from the surrounding society. Paul himself succumbed to that pressure, "which he probably did not find very important." The patriarchalization was already at work in the editing of the Christian Scriptures and in the selection of their canon.

Feminist scholars like Schüssler-Fiorenza are already more critical in their dealing with the Scripture than Latin American theologians. However, the overall enterprise of feminist theology goes much further, especially in criticizing the basic patriarchal paradigm. When they come to an awareness of the deep-seated patriarchy in Christianity, some women—indeed, some who, like Mary Daly, began as theologians—end up repudiating Christianity itself.

Rosemary Ruether, whose career has combined scholarship and activism, has written numerous works on both feminism and liberation theology. Her 1983 book *Sexism and God-Talk* is a systematic survey of traditional areas of theology from a feminist viewpoint. I would here like to cite some examples, primarily to show how fundamental the feminist critique of theology is.

Ruether traces how male images of the divine from the ancient Near East and the Bible itself buttress patriarchy in society. Patriarchy means "not only the subordination of females to males, but the whole structure of Father-ruled society: aristocracy over serfs, masters over slaves, king over subjects, racial overlords over colonized people."

Although patriarchal images predominate, "there are critical elements in Biblical theology that contradict this view of God." One source of a critique is Jesus' use of the term *Abba* ("father," but connoting great familiarity), which creates a new liberative community. "You are to call no man father, master or Lord." In Christian history there is an ambivalence, and "a host of new ecclesiastical and imperial 'holy fathers' arises, claiming the fatherhood and kingship of God as the basis of their power over others." Ruether says there must be different liberative images of God—or, as she says, of "God/ess," using a term that moves beyond an exclusively male image and can incorporate features of female deities. Although she recognizes the positive side of a parenting image of God, she believes overrelying on such an image reinforces patriarchalism; God becomes a neurotic parent who does not want human beings to grow up. She suggests a God of exodus, of liberation and new being, without following the route of "patriarchal" theologies of hope or liberation.

Ruether and others argue that an ecological-feminist theology must "rethink the whole Western theological tradition of the hierarchical chain of being and chain of command . . . the hierarchy of human over nonhuman nature as a relationship of ontological and moral value. It must challenge the right of the human to treat the nonhuman as private property and material wealth to be exploited."

> The God/ess who is primal Matrix, the ground of being-new being, is neither stifling immanence nor rootless transcendence. Spirit and matter are not dichotomized but are the inside and outside of the same thing.

In asking "Can a Male Savior Save Women?" Ruether emphasizes the prophetic and liberative side of Jesus' career, contrasting it to the patriarchalization of Christology during the next five centuries. She describes some alternatives, such as "androgynous Christologies" in the early Gnostics, Jacob Böhme, Emanuel Swedenborg, and utopian sects. Nevertheless, she finds that these approaches still tend toward an "androcentric bias." She concludes that, theologically speaking, "the maleness of Jesus has no ultimate significance." Jesus "manifests the *kenosis of patriarchy*" (*kenosis* is the Greek term for "emptying out" used to describe Jesus' manner of living and dying). "Jesus, the homeless Jewish prophet, and the marginalized women and men who respond to him represent the overthrowing of the present world system and the sign of a dawning new age in which God's will is done on earth."

Her vision of society is one of democratic socialism that dismantles sexist and class hierarchies and lives in organic community, with work and nurture shared. I should simply note that by contrast Latin American visions of a future society tend to focus more narrowly on economic restructuring. Ruether sees two routes toward such a society: establishing small communities that strive to put the concept into practice among themselves, and concentrating on more limited areas within the larger existing society. She does not even consider the theoretical possibility of "seizing state power" in order to set it in motion.

The radical thrust of Ruether's feminist theology is manifest in her reflections on "eschatology" (*eschata* is the Greek form for "last things," traditionally heaven, hell, judgment, etc.), the study of the destiny of the cosmos and of human beings. After a survey of eschatologies in the great religions, she takes up the critiques of both liberal evolutionary thought and Marxist millenarianism. She confronts the dilemma: if the "end" is "beyond," it offers nothing to history, but if the "end" is within history (e.g., a particular revolution), it will become absolutized. By holding out a transcendent end point beyond history, the Christian criticism of Marxism may be useful for keeping history open, but it has "no roots in an ontology of creation and in God/ess as ground of creation." She suggests instead a model of hope and change based on conversion, which would have "roots in nature and entail acceptance of finitude, human scale, and balanced relationships."

With regard to personal immortality Ruether proposes "agnosticism." "We should not pretend to know what we do not know or to have had 'revealed' to us what is the projection of our wishes. . . . What we know is that death is the cessation of the life process that holds our organism together." Our life "dissolves back into the cosmic matrix of matter/energy, from which new centers of . . . individuation arise. It is this matrix, rather than our individuated centers of being, that is 'everlasting.' " What makes this position feminist is Ruether's suspicion that the desire for immortality is primarily a male projection.

The foregoing are samples of the work of one feminist theologian, one of the most persistent and systematic in her approaches. What should be obvious is that her enterprise, while similar in many ways to the work of Latin Americans, is far more radical in its willingness to question not only distorted accretions in theology or church practice but the very symbols used by the Scriptures themselves. This radical approach reflects, I believe, the fact that patriarchy is more deep-seated than imperialism or class oppression, and much more structured into existing civilization.

12. DOES IT LIBERATE?

Objections to Liberation Theology

ITS OPPONENTS CHARGE THAT LIBERATION THEOLOGY RESTS ON faulty economic and political assumptions and analysis and leads to Marxist totalitarian dictatorship. They also say that it undermines church authority and falsifies the very meaning of Christianity. While such opponents tend to focus on one side or the other, they also cross lines. My aim here will be to summarize and examine the major objections, and the responses theologians make or might make. The discussion is already highly polemicized, and I do not aim to persuade anyone but simply to outline the contours of the controversy.

Although there are a number of critiques of liberation theology, such as those of Archbishop López Trujillo and James V. Schall, I have found it useful to consider mainly the economic and political critique developed by Michael Novak and some of his Latin American associates, and the theological critique developed by Cardinal Joseph Ratzinger.

Faulty Diagnosis?

Novak and his associates are primarily concerned with the economic and political framework utilized by liberation theologians. The theologians spend little time defending that framework, since it is widely accepted by Latin American intellectuals and since they see their task as theologians as that of reflecting on the implications of Christian faith. Nevertheless, if their social theory is fundamentally wrong, their whole enterprise is in jeopardy. Hence, the objections should at least be considered here.

There are in fact two basic questions: (1) How should the development of some nations, primarily in the West, and the poverty of others be explained? and (2) How can those countries that are poor today reach an adequate level of development?

In broad terms, answers have tended to be along two lines. Some see the rise of the West as primarily a matter of innovation, intelligence, and diligence, favored by the freedoms of an open society, while others stress the role of plunder and exploitation. In a parallel manner the task of development can be seen as primarily a matter of following in the footsteps of the presently developed countries under their tutelage, or as breaking free from their domination so as to be able to develop autonomously. Obviously, it is difficult to be "value-free" in such a discussion.

Although Novak strikes the pose of one who is questioning accepted wisdom, namely dependence theory, I find that he is simply restating what has been the conventional view of development all along. For example, he asks how Latin America and

North America, which until 1850 had comparable per capita incomes, could have evolved so differently, and focuses only on culture. "Latin Americans do not value the same moral qualities North Americans do." In their hostility to capitalism Catholics failed to grasp the secret of creating wealth. Sadly, he says, liberation theologians and bishops are repeating their error today when they assume that the wealth of others is the result of their own poverty.

There is an element of truth in this critique. One sometimes has the impression that Latin Americans believe that North American and European prosperity rests primarily on their exploitation of the Third World—as though the United States had developed nuclear weapons out of Central American bananas or space programs out of Peruvian fish meal. The prosperity of the advanced capitalist countries is due primarily to their own innovation and ever growing productivity since the onset of the industrial revolution in the middle of the eighteenth century.

That does not end the matter, however. How is the history of the last two and a half centuries to be explained? In reexamining their own histories Latin Americans see colonialism as having decisively shaped—or misshaped—their economies and institutions. Historically, their economies were organized around the export of minerals, hides, dyes, and so forth and that situation did not change with independence. The new nations continued to have plantation economies producing rubber, hemp, coffee, sugar, cotton, and so forth, often in boom-and-bust cycles. The United States, by contrast, was a society of small farmers, craft workers, and tradespeople—except in the South, where a similar plantation system was destroyed only by the Civil War.

When the Great Depression dramatically lowered the market for its exports, Latin America began a process of industrialization that lasted into the 1950s. This "import-substitution" kind of industry was led by Latin American entrepreneurs, with protectionist measures from the state. Large-scale penetration of foreign corporations and banks in the 1960s, however, meant that Latin American economies were "denationalized."

Latin Americans argue that underdevelopment is structural. Their economies are distorted by an "international division of labor" maintained by corporations of the capitalist world and their governments and elites. They cannot organize their economies to meet the basic needs of the people.

I believe it is possible to give due weight to both kinds of factors—that is, to understand underdevelopment as structural, without making dependence the primary factor explaining the prosperity of the industrialized nations (see, for example, *Europe and the People Without History* by the anthropologist-turned-historian Eric R. Wolf).

Economic Crisis

Novak has high words of praise for Joseph Ramos, an economist who has worked with the United Nations, and who served as a consultant to the Latin American bishops in preparation for Puebla. While he acknowledges dependence as a fact, Ramos adduces a number of elements to qualify it. First, he points out that Latin America's annual economic growth rate has averaged more than 5 percent for thirty years, that its industries have become increasingly sophisticated and competitive, and that statistics show a rise in general welfare (e.g., from the 1940s to the 1970s life expectancy increased from less than fifty years to sixty-two years).

What has to be done now, according to Ramos, is to raise the standard of living of the poorest. Two of his colleagues have calculated that the bottom 40 percent could be brought above the "poverty line" (less than $200 a year annual income) by an expenditure of $16 billion a year. That amount would be equivalent to 5 percent of the GNP or 22 percent of present (late 1970s) government spending. By developing the internal market such a redistribution would serve the interests of domestic manufacturers.

As rational as such a proposal might sound considered abstractly, it ignores the way power is used by Latin American elites. A serious redistribution of income supposes a redistribution of power—which is the essence of revolution.

For his part Novak proposes that Latin America take its cue from the example of Asian countries like Japan, Taiwan, Singapore, Hong Kong, Malaysia, and South Korea. He ignores the fact that Japan closed its borders to the West until its own industrialization was underway. By early in this century it was an industrialized country, and in 1941 it was powerful enough to presume to attack the United States. Its postwar recovery was similar to that of Europe's and is not directly applicable to the Third World. In Japan and Taiwan, moreover, an imposed land reform sped up capitalist industrialization.

Without gainsaying the entrepreneurial ability, ingenuity, and thrift in the countries Novak cites, the fact is that all these are cases of enclave economies, primarily export platforms that supply cheap labor at particular stages of internationalized production processes. In some cases local entrepreneurs have extended the process—e.g., in Korea, which now has its own automobile industry. Nevertheless, such a model is of very limited applicability. In the mid-1980s there is little evidence that the world economy has room for many more Taiwans.

Finally, the economic picture has changed since the late 1970s when Ramos made his optimistic assumptions. Today Latin America is in its worst economic crisis since the 1930s. Servicing the foreign debt ($360 billion) consumes 40 percent of the continent's exports. In some countries, such as Peru, living standards have fallen back to the levels of twenty years ago. Latin America produces less food per capita than it did forty years ago. These and other indicators reinforce the basic thrust of the dependency critique, that Latin American poverty is structural and can be overcome only by basic structural changes.

Cuba a Failure?

For Novak as for others, the Cuba argument clinches the case. Cuba, they say, is a totalitarian society, is dependent on the Soviet Union, and has not performed well economically. Any similar attempts by other Latin American countries will only worsen their situation.

The validity of liberation theology does not depend on an evaluation of Cuba. New efforts at basic change need not follow the Cuban model. Latin Americans believe that they can learn from others' experiences, including those of Cuba, and yet work out new models appropriate to their own circumstances.

Cuba has eliminated the dire poverty that existed prior to the revolution. The whole population of Cuba has an adequate diet, is able to work, and has access to medical care and schooling. That is true of no other Latin American country. Critics ignore or downplay that achievement. By contrast, the fact that elsewhere large sectors of the population, often the majority, are unemployed or underemployed and do not have an adequate diet or access to regular health care is considered incidental.

A few statistical indicators may suggest that Cuba is not the "failure" it is often assumed to be. On the "physical quality of life" index (a composite of infant mortality, life expectancy, and literacy) Cuba scores 84—as opposed to the Latin American average of 71 and the industrialized Western countries' average of over 90. The only Latin American country to surpass Cuba is Argentina (85), which has twice Cuba's per capita income. Similarly, although Brazil's average per capita income ($702) is higher than Cuba's ($598), the bottom 80 percent of Cuban society has a higher income.

Is there a trade-off between certain undeniable accomplishments in material welfare and the sacrifice of basic freedoms and rights? Again, matters look different depending on the observer's viewpoint. Brazil's freedom of the press contrasts with Cuba's government monopoly. Yet what benefit do the poor majority of Brazilians derive from the free press, especially the illiterate? In theory, anyone can publish a newspaper or apply for a TV license. In practice, the media are in the hands of the wealthy and present constant images of a consumer society that can only tantalize the poor majority. Even admitting the dangers and pathologies of a one-party state, is it not at least conceivable that—when seen from the viewpoint of the poor—the Cuban system with its forms of local participation is at least as accountable and democratic as the Brazilian political system? How "democratic" is a society where all the mechanisms are in place—parties, elections, Congress—but no serious proposals for reform are allowed on the agenda?

These considerations by no means answer all the objections to liberation theology on economic or political grounds, but simply indicate that I do not regard such objections as unanswerable.

The "Ratzinger Letter"

As noted in Chapter Six, systematic attack on liberation theology within the church began around 1972. It is simplistic to assume that this opposition is a reflection of an alliance between bishops and oligarchs. Liberation theology challenges the church's overall understanding of itself as well as individual roles church leaders should play. Yet that challenge comes not from a direct attack on the church or on doctrine. Indeed, in doctrinal expression Latin American liberation theologians are more conservative than many Catholic liberals in Europe and North America. The challenge comes from a way of doing theology in which the starting point is the situation of the poor.

The so-called "Ratzinger letter" ("Instruction on Certain Aspects of the Theology of Liberation," issued in August 1984) is a compendium of the major objections to liberation theology from an ecclesiastical viewpoint. Once a progressive theologian, Ratzinger was active in the preparation of Vatican II. During the postcouncil period he apparently concluded that matters had gotten out of hand and that church authority had to be reasserted.

The first half of the seven-thousand-word document deals with general considerations about liberation, the Bible, and church authority, while the second part is directed to criticizing Marxist analysis, the use of violence, the concept of the church, and the kind of hermeneutics used in liberation theology. Unlike overtly right-wing critics, Ratzinger does not simply condemn liberation theology. The opening words are "The Gospel of Jesus Christ is a message of freedom and a force for liberation. In recent years this essential truth has become the object of reflection for theologians, with a new kind of attention which is itself full of promise." The aim of the letter is to draw attention "to the deviations and risks of deviation . . . that are brought about by certain forms of liberation theology which use, in an insufficiently critical manner, concepts borrowed from various currents of Marxist thought."

Ratzinger speaks of "theologies" of liberation—in other words, in the plural. This strategem, which Bishop López Trujillo began in the early 1970s, implies that there are acceptable and unacceptable varieties of liberation theology. Since no names are named, it is impossible to determine who is indeed regarded as acceptable. The theologians themselves—Gutiérrez, Segundo, Dussel, Sobrino, the Boffs, Assmann, Ellacuría, Vidales, Comblin, Richard, Muñoz—may differ in style and approach and may disagree on some issues, but they refer to liberation theology in the singular, since they see their own efforts as supporting what is essentially a single historical process. At first glance, it might be assumed that the "deviations" are the work of minor figures, perhaps individual priests carried away by rhetoric. However, the fact that Ratzinger's Congregation summoned both Gutiérrez and Leonardo Boff to Rome would indicate otherwise. If the central figures have "deviated," one is left wondering who the acceptable liberation theologians are.

In an early paragraph Ratzinger aserts that "liberation is *first and foremost* liberation from the radical slavery of sin. . . . As a *logical consequence,* it calls for freedom from many different kinds of slavery in the cultural, economic, social and political spheres, all of which derive ultimately from sin." The problem, according to the document, is that some place a one-sided emphasis on "liberation from servitude of an earthly and temporal kind" and "seem to put liberation from sin in second place." This passage is a clear expression of the "dualism" so often criticized by Latin American theologians. Elsewhere the document states:

> Structures, whether they are good or bad, are the result of man's actions, and so are consequences more than causes. The root of evil, then, lies in free and responsible persons who have to be converted by the grace of Jesus Christ. . . . [IV, 15]

Perhaps the most radical statement of this dualism comes in a paragraph on the Psalms: "It is from God alone that one can expect salvation and healing. God, and not man, has the power to change the situations of suffering" (IV, 5).

Ratzinger repeatedly accuses liberation theology of a "reductionism" that ignores basic elements of Christianity: of reducing sin to social structures, of making the struggle for justice the whole essence of salvation, of reducing the gospel to a purely earthly gospel, of equating truth with partisan praxis, of denying "the transcendent character of the distinction between good and evil (IV, 15; VI, 4; VIII, 3–5; VIII,9). When theologians criticize dualism they are reflecting "historicist immanentism." The growth of the kingdom of God is mistakenly identified with human liberation—"self-redemption" through class struggle.

In their initial reactions most Latin American theologians claimed that the Ratzinger document did not apply to them and that what it described was a caricature of liberation theology. In a number of articles they even welcomed the document as a contribution to dialogue and agreed that the kinds of positions the instruction described would deserve censure. Juan Luis Segundo, however, was convinced that the document was indeed attacking the enterprise of Latin American theology itself. In reply he published a small book, *Theology and the Church: A Response to Cardinal Ratzinger and a Warning to the Whole Church*.

Segundo insists that a crucial point of contention is the nature of human activity. As pointed out in Chapter Five, liberation theology insists that there are not two histories, profane and sacred, but only one human history, which is a history of salvation. Segundo points to various texts from Vatican II and a key gospel passage in Matthew 25, Jesus' parable of the last judgment ("I was hungry and you gave me food."). The implication is that people are saved by what they *do* for others, independently of how explicitly "religious" their intentions.

To buttress his case Segundo recalls that Pope Paul VI, in closing the council, asked rhetorically whether the council might not have "deviated" by accepting the "anthropocentric positions of modern culture." The pope immediately replied, "Deviated, no; turned, yes" and stressed the "intimate union . . . between human and temporal values and . . . spiritual, religious and eternal values."

Segundo is in effect saying that those who, like Ratzinger, attack liberation theology have not realized the full implication of what was declared at Vatican II. He adds that if Ratzinger is right, he (Segundo) is wrong and has been wrong for twenty-five years—as has the whole post-Vatican II generation of theologians and bishops. It is unusual—practically unheard of—for a Latin American theologian to engage in such head-on polemics with a major Vatican figure.

Both Ratzinger and Segundo can support their position with official church texts. What is clear is that official Catholic teaching now holds that there is a very close connection between salvation and efforts to build a more human world. Despite terminological variation—is work for justice a "constitutive dimension" of preaching the gospel or simply an "integral part?"—the Catholic church has accepted a major tenet of liberation theology. Segundo is drawing attention to the implications of this official position.

Where It Leads

Toward the end of the first half of the document, Ratzinger refers to a kind of liberation theology that "proposes a novel interpretation of both the content of faith and of Christian existence which seriously departs from the faith of the church and, in fact, actually constitutes a practical negation" (VI, 9).

Bureaucratic phraseology may obscure the import of this statement. Cardinal Ratzinger, the church official whose responsibility it is to protect Catholic teaching, is saying that liberation theology is unorthodox. He attributes its errors, which affect both doctrinal and moral teaching, to concepts "uncritically borrowed from Marxist ideology" and to a biblical hermeneutics "marked by rationalism." The new interpretation is "corrupting whatever was authentic in the initial commitment on behalf of the poor."

The second half of the document seeks to show the consequences of liberation theology. Ratzinger takes up the use of Marxist analysis, and the notion of praxis, and moves into the theological consequences of such an analysis. He also highlights liberation theology's critique of the church and its method of biblical interpretation. A final section titled "Orientations" aims to present positive suggestions but in fact returns to the attack. Many of the topics Ratzinger takes up have already been treated in the course of this book.

From his remark about "uncritical" borrowing from Marxism one might assume that some form of "critical" borrowing might be acceptable, but the whole anti-Marxist tenor of the document nullifies that possibility.

Most of Ratzinger's argument is more epistemological than

theological—that is, he is questioning Marxism's approach to understanding reality rather than its impact on Christian faith. He asserts that in "human and social sciences it is well to be aware above all of the plurality of methods and viewpoints," since reality is complex. Marxism, however, proposes "such a global vision that data are brought together into a philosophical and ideological structure, which predetermines the significance and importance to be attached to them. . . . Thus no separation of the parts of this epistemologically unique complex is possible. If one tries to take only one part, say, the analysis, one ends up having to accept the entire ideology" (VII, 6). Ratzinger here seems to be attempting to reverse the cautious but real acceptance of Christians practicing "discernment" with regard to socialism and Marxism on the part of Pope Paul VI in his encyclical *Octogesima Adveniens* (1971).

Like the reductionism mentioned above, this conviction about Marxist epistemology is central to Ratzinger's view. One cannot take even a few steps into the waves without being seized and swept away by a riptide.

This "all-embracing conception" has serious consequences for ethics. In the logic of Marxist thought, analysis "is inseparable from the praxis and from the conception of history to which this praxis is linked." Only by being involved as a partisan in struggle can one work out the analysis correctly. "There is no truth, they [Marxists] pretend, except in and through partisan praxis." This means class struggle, which is "the fundamental law of history." Since society is founded on violence, the only recourse is the "counterviolence of the revolution." In entering the struggle, which is itself "an objective, necessary law" one " 'makes' truth." There is no point in appealing to ethical motivation. Indeed,

> the very nature of ethics is radically called into question because of the borrowing of these theses from Marxism. In fact it is the transcendent character of the distinction between good and evil, the principle of morality, which is implicitly denied in the perspective of the class struggle. [VIII, 9]

In taking up the theological consequences of borrowing from Marxism, Ratzinger again warns that "we are facing . . . a real system, even if some hesitate to follow the logic to its conclusion." In denying "the distinction between the history of salvation and profane history," liberation theology tends to "identify the kingdom of God and its growth with the human liberation movement." History becomes "a process of the self-redemption of man by means of the class struggle." Faith, hope, and charity "are given a new content . . . 'fidelity to history'. . . ." Liberation theology maintains that it is an illusion to suppose that one can love one's class enemies. Universal love will become possible only after the revolution [IX, 1,3,5,7].

The conception of the church also comes under fire. Here Ratzinger says liberation theology questions whether Christians who belong to different social classes should share in the same Eucharist. For Ratzinger this example seems to epitomize what is objectionable, since he mentions it in two other passages. Liberation theology's reductionism takes the mystery out of the church, making it simply "a reality interior to history." It also makes "a disastrous confusion between the poor of the Scripture and the proletariat of Marx." The "church of the poor" really means a class church.

In their critique of the church liberation theologians are said to question not simply the behavior of its pastors but the "sacramental and hierarchical structure of the church, which was willed by the Lord himself." Bishops are regarded as "objective representatives of the ruling class." The theologians are said to hold that church leaders "take their origin from the people, who therefore designate ministers of their own choice in accord with the needs of their historic revolutionary mission." This notion of ministers taking their origin from the people strongly hints at a Protestant theology of ministry. Ratzinger perhaps probably has in mind Leonardo Boff, since it is he who has written most forthrightly on church structures.

As Ratzinger begins to wind up his argument, shorthand phrases fly faster, rising to a crescendo pitch: "temporal messianism," "class eucharist," "reductionist reading of the Bible," "the most radical theses of rationalist exegesis," and traditional creeds being given a "new meaning . . . which is a negation of the faith of the church."

In closing, Ratzinger warns that the document should not be taken as some kind of "approval . . . of those who keep the poor in misery." Church people should struggle for human rights, but

> this battle must be fought in ways consistent with human dignity. That is why the systematic and deliberate recourse to blind violence, no matter from which side it comes, must be condemned. To put one's trust in violent means in the hope of restoring more justice is to become the victim of a fatal illusion: Violence begets violence and degrades man. It mocks the dignity of man in the person of the victims, and it debases that same dignity among those who practice it.

This is his most explicit rejection of revolutionary violence, although the notion is implicit earlier.

While Ratzinger recognizes that the structures that "conceal poverty . . . are themselves forms of violence," he asserts that "it is only by making an appeal to the moral potential of the person and to the constant need for interior conversion" that any social change will be really beneficial.

Ratzinger warns against illusionary anticipations about revolution:

> A major fact of our times ought to evoke the reflection of all those who would sincerely work for the true liberation of their brothers: Millions of our own contemporaries legitimately yearn to recover those basic freedoms of which they were deprived by totalitarian and atheistic regimes which came to power by violent and revolutionary means, precisely in the name of the liberation of the people. This shame of our time cannot be ignored: While claiming to bring them freedom, these regimes keep whole nations in conditions of servitude which are unworthy of mankind. Those who, perhaps inadvertently, make themselves accomplices of similar enslavements betray the very poor they mean to help. [XI, 10]

The rather condescending tone implies that Latin American theologians need a history lesson from a European.

Ratzinger concludes with yet one more recital of what must be emphasized, "the transcendence and gratuity of liberation in Jesus Christ," and so forth. One sentence summarizes much of the theological case against liberation theology:

> One needs to be on guard against the politicization of existence which, misunderstanding the entire meaning of the kingdom of God and the transcendence of the person, begins to sacralize politics and betray the religion of the people in favor of the projects of the revolution.

Ratzinger's critique is itself a highly condensed summary of more than a dozen years of criticism within the Latin American church. Readers can judge whether his description fits liberation theology as presented throughout the present work, and indeed, which account they find more adequate. My observations in the next few pages will only draw attention to some weaknesses in Ratzinger's position when seen from that of liberation theology.

Ratzinger paints a picture of liberation theologians swept away by an all-embracing system, and insists, on the contrary, that the ultimate criterion of truth must be theological. His position—one frequently found in official church documents—is that faith enables one to rise above ideologies. (Curiously, being an American also seems to raise one above ideology. In the 1950s sociologist Daniel Bell proclaimed the "end of ideology.") Latin American theologians are skeptical. Ideology is already embedded in any culture, and in language itself. Juan Luis Segundo explicitly states that Jesus, in sharing the human condition, also took on the ideological elements of his time, and they are reflected in the New Testament. To be above ideology one would have to be above the human condition.

In this view the alternatives are not whether we do or do not use ideological elements but whether we use them uncritically or self-critically. Thus, a Latin American theologian might say,

"Yes, it is true we 'borrow' some elements from Marxism, but we do so consciously and critically. That is better than unconsciously absorbing the ideological elements from the dominant Western capitalist culture and imagining that one is above ideology." Not even Vatican officials or the pope can rise above ideology.

One point where I sympathize with Ratzinger is in his rejection of the "scientific" character of Marxism. In part, the problem is terminological, since both Romance and Germanic languages use "science" in a broader sense than is customary in English. Even making room for a wider definition of "science," I am left uncomfortable with the notion that Marxism is a "science of history" and that "bourgeois" social science is really "prescientific," as though Marx were the (not yet fully acknowledged) Copernicus of the social sciences. However, even those liberation theologians who speak of Marxism as science explicitly recognize the need to pay attention to other currents, and do so in practice.

Do liberation theologians accept Marxism as an all-embracing system to the exclusion of other sources of insight and knowledge? A simple examination of sources cited by Gutiérrez, Segundo, Boff, Dussel, and others indicates that they in fact draw on a spectrum of approaches. Many of them, such as Sobrino, cite primarily other theologians. In discussing liberation theology's use of the Marxist tradition, Leonardo Boff mentions Antonio Gramsci and Louis Althusser in the same phrase, even though they stand close to opposite poles in the question of how "humanist" or "antihumanist" Marx himself was.

Indeed, one could conclude that Latin American theologians, far from having made a systematic and coherent adaptation of Marxism have rather made eclectic use of elements from it, with little concern for a coherent total system. With a few exceptions they have not engaged in an explicit, head-on confrontation with Marxism. In asserting that one cannot pick and choose, that even using Marxist analysis will inevitably make one captive of a whole system with all the consequences he spells out, Ratzinger is saying that he understands what they are doing better than they do themselves.

Again, I can partly sympathize with Ratzinger's rejection of a notion of "praxis" that holds up partisan involvement as the unique source of truth in all matters and for all time. Although one might find some such expressions among enthusiasts, they do not represent the considered view of liberation theologians. That is, involvement in the struggle of the poor cannot substitute for the properly intellectual work of theology. Clodovis Boff makes that point explicit in his work on methodology, *Teologia e Praxis*. Yet I am impelled to ask: who is more likely to understand the situation of the Brazilian peasant, in human terms, in social analysis, theologically and pastorally—an individual who supervises a doctrinal watchdog agency in the Vatican, or a theologian who teaches half the year in a Brazilian university and spends the other half year trekking into roadless sections of the Amazon basin, as does Clodovis Boff? All things being equal, one assumes that Boff's face-to-face contact with peasants and sharing in their lives and doing pastoral work—his praxis—sharpens his own awareness, provides a testing ground for his study of social sciences and for his theology itself, and stimulates him to raise new questions. In principle, of course, all things might not be equal. Sipping espresso in a Roman piazza, Ratzinger might come to an insight that eludes Boff as he slogs through the jungle with blistered feet and infected mosquito bites. In the ordinary run of things, however, Boff's pastoral practice will have a positive impact on his intellectual work.

Ratzinger echoes others who, perhaps with priest-guerrillas in mind, believe liberation theology seeks to provide a rationale for revolutionary violence. In fact, no theologian has written a book on the issue. No liberation theologian has provided a theological rationale for killing. To the extent death is theologized, it is in reflections on martyrdom, the willingness to give one's life for others, not to take others' lives.

The structure of Ratzinger's thinking indicates that he sees violence as due to outsiders, including church people, who convince unsuspecting poor people that they must take up class struggle. The fact is that no one can induce revolution—as Che Guevara and his followers found in 1967 in Bolivia. When ordinary people turn to violence, it is generally a last resort and in their minds is essentially self-defense. In any case, it does not derive from liberation theology.

For almost twenty years some Latin Americans have been searching for a form of active nonviolence apt for Latin America. While they admire the historical examples of Gandhi, Martin Luther King, and others, they are quite convinced that they cannot simply import those experiences. The Nobel Prize winner Adolfo Pérez Esquivel was the first continent-wide secretary of a nonviolent network, largely church based, called Servicio Justicia y Paz.

In 1984 Cardinal Arns of São Paulo wrote a memorandum to the United States peace movement stating that liberation theology is the "ideological basis" for Latin American nonviolence and inquiring what the equivalent would be in the United States. In other words, contrary to the prevailing stereotype, Cardinal Arns sees liberation theology as providing a basis for an explicit commitment to nonviolence.

Ratzinger states that Marxism assumes that society is "built on violence," either the violence of the present order or revolutionary violence. Segundo counters that one should not assume that the United States or France is built on violence because they underwent revolutions.

In *Faith and Ideologies* Segundo develops at considerable length his idea that guerrilla warfare and the reaction it provokes destroy the social "ecology" of a society. By ecology he means the whole series of relationships existing among human beings and between them and their environment. His sober discussion is far from any romanticizing of revolutionary violence.

As Ratzinger mentions to his evident distaste, some liberation theologians do raise questions about the Eucharist in a class society. Clearly, the first generation of Christians saw the

Eucharist as a celebration of brother- and sisterhood in the Lord. Paul reprimands the Corinth community because when they meet there are divisions and factions and some go hungry while others even get drunk (1 Cor.:11). Over the centuries the Eucharist took on features of imperial court pageantry that obscured the original meaning of the Lord's Supper.

Let us suppose a mass celebrated in the presence of generals and colonels who share responsibility for the torture and death of hundreds or even thousands of civilians. Or let us suppose a mass in a parish in a wealthy neighborhood of a capital city, where the average per capita income is fifty times that of the peasants who form the lower half of the population. If in such cases the mass serves to tranquilize consciences, does it not falsify the symbolism? On the other hand, if a group of peasants is growing in a sense of solidarity with one another and responsibility for each other, is it not understandable that the Eucharist would be experienced as a celebration of sister- and brotherhood? And if there is a celebration across class lines, should it not express a yearning for a society of fundamental equality? Latin American theologians do not say that eucharistic celebration should be suspended until the dawn of a new society but simply that respect for the Eucharist demands that its symbolism not be falsified. By the same token it is incorrect to assert, as Ratzinger does, that liberation theologians deny the "sacramentality" of the church (see Chapter Ten). As this instance shows, they are concerned that the church really be a "sacrament"—that is, a sign—of the presence of Christ in the world.

In asserting that liberation theology questions the hierarchical nature of the church, Ratzinger no doubt wants to liken it to the kind of challenge raised by European and American theologians, such as the Swiss Hans Küng. Liberation theologians, however, have clearly tried to distinguish themselves from even "progressive" European and American theologians. A comparison may be helpful. In its essentials Küng's critique of prevailing Roman Catholic ecclesiology comes down to this: from the New Testament writings we can see that Jesus himself did not found a church, but rather his life and death (and by faith, his resurrection) set in motion a movement which over the course of time took on increasingly institutional forms. If the present forms of church office, such as bishop and priest, do not derive from Jesus himself, then there is room for other varieties. For example, there is no biblical reason for excluding women from any church offices. Similarly, Küng and others question papal infallibility, saying that it has no basis in Scripture and that it is built on an inadequate concept of truth.

Such a line of thought is clearly threatening to the whole system of the Roman church, at least as seen from the Vatican. It is understandable why Rome should declare that Küng no longer teaches Catholic doctrine and prohibit Catholic institutions from employing him. Nevertheless, many theologians teaching in Catholic theology departments hold similar positions.

No doubt many Latin American theologians agree with the thrust of Küng's critique on scholarly grounds. Nevertheless, they have refrained from taking up such a banner, and their own ecclesiology can be regarded as doctrinally conservative. For example, in his book replying to the Ratzinger instruction, Juan Luis Segundo explicitly accepts the Catholic notion of a 'magisterium," that is, the official teaching authority vested in the pope and the bishops. Part of his argument is that the teaching authority of Vatican II, which he believes he is following, is greater than that of Ratzinger's office.

The Latin American critique that comes closest to Küng's is Leonardo Boff's book *Church: Charism and Power*. However, Boff's primary concern is that the church really be a church of the poor. Unlike most of his Latin American colleagues, he raises the issue of human rights *within* the church. At one point he quotes at great length a Brazilian lay Catholic who makes a point-by-point parallel between Kremlin and Vatican styles of governance (e.g., the pope and the general secretary of the Communist Party of the USSR, the Roman curia and the Politburo). His aim is not to question the principle of hierarchical authority, but to critique, from the standpoint of the gospel call to serve the poor, its way of operating.

Ratzinger's church is largely hierarchical and clerical. His class assumptions become astonishingly transparent when he asserts that "the church needs competent people from a scientific and technological viewpoint, as well as in the human and political science" for putting its "social teaching" into effect, and then in an adjoining paragraph asserts that liberation theology is "popularized" in base communities that are unable to exercise any "discernment" or "critical judgement." By this logic pastors should take their cue in political matters from (middle-class) lay experts but should teach "discernment" to (poor) members of base communities. The social theorists with whom Ratzinger disagrees are ipso facto incompetent, and the poor have nothing to teach the clergy or the privileged.

More than once Ratzinger insists that his criticisms should not comfort those who oppress the poor, and he briefly denounced oligarchies, military dictatorships, and the violation of human rights. His position is that "hearts" must be converted before structures are changed; he rejects the opposite position, that structures must be changed first, as materialistic. Liberation theologians do not believe that structures must be changed first. Rather, their experience is that "hearts" are converted as people join together in solidarity to struggle for a more just world.

Ratzinger's recipe for society at large is the church's "social doctrine." That doctrine, laid out in the writings of popes in recent decades, has given rise to diverse interpretations and seems ambiguous. In the 1930s Pius XI's vision seemed so close to corporativism that dictators, like Getúlio Vargas in Brazil and Juan Domingo Perón in Argentina, could invoke it. More recently, Christian Democratic parties have claimed to take inspiration from it and have received direct and indirect support from bishops, although they have sought to insist on their independence from the hierarchy. Donal Dorr entitles his history of the social doctrine *Option for the Poor*, while Michael Novak, in *Freedom With Justice,* believes the same body of doctrine points toward his own vision of democratic capitalism, though not necessarily so. Does the "social doctrine" have in mind a particular model of society? It denounces both capitalism and socialism in their present forms. Does it envision a hybrid form, or does it logically lead to some form of communitarian anarchism? Invoking the church's "social teaching" plainly does not end the discussion.

Since its inception, liberation theology has been controversial. Theologians devote a good part of their energy to replying to objections, whether explicit or implicit. The discussion is more than academic, however, since they are defending the legitimacy of the liberating model of pastoral work. Nor will rationality alone settle the controversies. Behind the particular points at issue stand deeply opposed mind-sets, just as opponents and defenders of "Star Wars" line up according to their basic views of the world.

Any resolution will be found in practice, as Latin American Christians continue to struggle for a more just and humane society.

13. LOOKING AHEAD

Futurology is an impossible enterprise. What is certain about the future is that it will bring surprises. With that in mind I end this book with some modest observations on the further implications of liberation theology.

First, however, it would be worthwhile to summarize the impact liberation theology has already had during the last twenty years. Many Latin Americans have found in it a key for understanding their lives and destinies in biblical terms. They find a renewed sense of what Christianity means. Many have been murdered for daring to act on the implications of faith as they understand it. Prior to the intellectual work of the theologians is this reality of suffering and struggle.

One sign that their intellectual work was reaching a degree of maturity was the publication in 1985 of the first volumes of the Liberation and Theology series. At the start of the decade the Chilean theologian Sergio Torres and others believed it was time to present a systematic summation of Latin American theology, similar to encyclopedic works of classical theology. About forty theologians, virtually all those who have published significant materials, have participated in planning meetings and have accepted writing responsibilities. Most of the more than fifty volumes are being coauthored.

The initial topics are grouped around the title "Experience of God in the Struggle for Justice," and are followed by titles relating to classical theological themes: revelation, God, Jesus Christ, Spirit, Trinity, creation and history, sin and conversion, the church, sacraments, Mary, and so forth. Other volumes deal with questions of politics, human rights, evangelizing in a class society, economics (including a volume on the pastoral and theological aspects of land), and particular groups: women, Indians, and Afro-Americans.

It remains to be seen whether this work will break new ground or is primarily a consolidation and codification of work already done. It is of course quite possible that the Latin American theologians have in fact reached a kind of plateau and that they will have relatively little new to say in the immediate future. If that is the case, I suspect it will reflect the overall situation in Latin America. During the 1960s revolutionary change seemed to be underway. What actually took place, however, was counterrevolution, embodied in the military dictatorships of the 1970s. Most of these have since given way to civilian governments, which nevertheless are not capable of bringing about the basic structural changes needed. Hence, there is a kind of impasse. It would not be surprising if liberation theology reflected this impasse.

One obvious question is the future of this theology within the Catholic church. Certainly, the Vatican's attempts to rein in theologians like Boff and Gutiérrez indicate serious tension. Nevertheless, as I have been pointing out in this book, much of what is central to liberation theology is enshrined in official

Catholic teaching (Vatican II, Medellín, the bishops' synods of 1971 and 1974, and Puebla). Certain positions seem irreversible: that there is a close link between liberation and salvation; that the church must make an option for the poor; that no defense of freedom or "Christian" civilization can legitimize the murder of those who stand up to defend their rights; that full respect for human rights, including the right to employment and food, will demand a new kind of society—these and similar notions are part of official Catholic teaching.

Certain issues remain controversial: the use of Marxist categories, the proper role of the church in the political sphere, the place of base communities in the church as a whole. Such questions cannot be settled by fiat. Even if, for example, church authorities continue to warn against the use of Marxist categories, the underlying problems will not evaporate. A small group of people will still have disproportionate wealth and power over the rest of society whether they are called capitalists or business people, entrepreneurs or oligarchs.

Church authorities may be able to limit the impact of liberation theology by downplaying the import of what has already become official teaching and by qualifying it with another kind of discourse ("communion and participation" as opposed to "liberation"). Moreover, a consistent policy of appointing conservatives as bishops and maintaining a tight control over seminaries might well assure that the radicalized sectors of the clergy and hierarchy remain a minority.

Nevertheless, my own intuition is that events themselves are likely to outrun such strategies. Many Latin Americans believe that their current struggles are nothing less than a "second independence": in struggling for liberation they are taking up the unfinished business of their own origins as nations. Nevertheless, the form of such struggles cannot be determined beforehand. The Nicaraguan revolution may inspire Brazilians but it provides no model for their own work of liberation.

Despite the sense of impasse, these Latin Americans are convinced that history is on their side. Genuine development is impossible in the present world order. The present crisis, exemplified in the foreign debt, is but a manifestation of a long-range crisis that will be resolved only through a struggle both within their own countries and internationally. That struggle is economic, but it is also political, social, and cultural.

An analogy may help. Women in the Catholic church are demanding an end to male monopoly on power and authority. Their demand for equality is expressed in the movement for access to ordination to the priesthood. At a deeper level it is a critique of all patriarchy in the church. There is now something of a scholarly consensus that there is no legitimate scriptural or theological reason for excluding women from ordination. The Vatican and the bishops, while making occasional statements about the role of women in the church, have steadfastly refused to consider ordination. The issue will not go away, however, for the fact is that over one half of the church is made up of women. Indeed, women do considerably more than half of the church's everyday work.

Church authorities may make statements and take disciplinary actions, but not even the pope can decree away the fact that the vast majority of Latin Americans suffer from poverty. Hence, the issues raised by liberation and feminist theology will not go away.

From this perspective Latin American liberation theology—however important in itself—is but one aspect of a much larger movement, the emergence of the excluded—women, non-whites, the poor—onto the stage of history. Its fate is inseparably bound up with that larger movement.

Liberation theology is having a rebound impact on the United States. At almost any public action in protest of U.S. policy in Central America, half or more of the participants have become involved through church organizations. Some of the major initiatives have come from religious groups. The initial jolt was the March 1980 murder of Archbishop Romero (later revealed to have been carried out by individuals who were to become Nicaraguan *contras*), followed by the rape-murder of the U.S.

churchwomen in December of that year. Churches have taken in Central American refugees fleeing the violence in their countries, which is augmented by U.S. policy. When the U.S. government, ignoring international refugee law, began to target Central American refugees for deportation, a church in Tucson declared itself a public sanctuary. Since that time over three hundred congregations around the United States, supported by many more, have declared sanctuary. As a result, many Americans have been able to meet Salvadorans and Guatemalans and hear their experiences firsthand. Over two thousand people have gone to Nicaragua in Witness for Peace delegations to give nonviolent witness to their opposition to U.S. policy. Church people were also the core organizers of the Pledge of Resistance, a kind of preemptive mobilization of more than eighty thousand people ready to engage in massive demonstrations and civil disobedience in the event of a U.S. invasion or other major escalation in Central America. In such solidarity efforts people find that their own religious faith is deepened.

I have described liberation theology as

1. An interpretation of Christian faith out of the suffering, struggle, and hope of the poor.
2. A theological critique of society and its ideological underpinnings.
3. A critique of the practice of the church and of Christians.

That kind of endeavor is certainly not limited to Latin America, as is clear in the case of feminist, black, and Third World theologies. Can something similar take place within the mainstream U.S. churches? As I have suggested, behind the involvement of the churches in supporting Central American refugees and opposing U.S. Central American policy, there is already something like liberation theology at work.

Indeed, I think the pastoral letters of the U.S. Catholic bishops on nuclear weapons and on the U.S. economy can be read as the functional equivalents of the 1968 Medellín documents in Latin America. Certainly, there are important differences. The bishops' documents are the result of a far more extensive consultation and they incorporate the experience of the post-Vatican II generation of Catholics.

The bishops see their letter on peace as a starting point for a "theology of peace" that they see as yet to be developed. Such a theology would draw on "biblical studies, systematic and moral theology, ecclesiology, and the experience and insights of members of the church who have struggled in various ways to make and keep the peace in this often violent age." They go on to say that such a theology should

> ground the task of peacemaking solidly in the biblical vision of the kingdom of God, then place it centrally in the ministry of the church. It should specify the obstacles in the way of peace, as these are understood theologically and in the social and political sciences. It should both identify the specific contributions a community of faith can make to the work of peace and relate these to the wider work of peace pursued by other groups and institutions in society. Finally, a theology of peace must include a message of hope.

Substituting the word "liberation" for "peace" would yield a good description of the theology I have been outlining in this book.

Many of the themes the U.S. bishops emphasize are central to liberation theology: the unity of the human family, the dignity of each individual, the idolatry of the "quest for unrestrained power and the desire for great wealth." The bishops state that "as individuals and as a nation . . . we are called to make a fundamental 'option for the poor,' " and they say that any economy should be evaluated in terms of its impact on the poor.

I do not mean to co-opt the Catholic bishops for liberation

theology. They explicitly state that they do not intend to question the U.S. economic system as such but merely to point to areas that need further development—a "new American experiment" to extend democracy to the economic sphere. Much of what they say calls for further development. For example, I think it is incumbent on the church to question seriously the pathological anti-Sovietism that is endemic in American culture. In the same vein, I think it is important to ask how the churches have coexisted peacefully with nuclear weapons from 1945 to the early 1980s and to examine the cultural and social effects of being citizens of a superpower. To what extent, in other words, have we so internalized our possession of nuclear weapons that they are part of our identity and we would feel naked and exposed without them? Is there not a connection between the United States' possession of the ultimate threat and its willingness to bully tiny, impoverished Central American countries? I believe such questions have a religious dimension and are implicit in the kind of further development the bishops call for.

What I most want to stress, however, is that I see an affinity between Latin American liberation theology and these pastoral letters. The fact that Michael Novak felt called to publish a critique of the letter on nuclear weapons that occupied a whole issue of *National Review* and that he headed a lay committee to respond to the letter on the economy confirms my intuition.

The pastoral letters, like Medellín, Puebla, and liberation theology, then, are a response to a deep question within Christian believers: what implication—if any—does Christian faith have for the great social challenges of the late twentieth century?

Some believers maintain that religion is indeed an interior matter and has no impact in the larger public world. For their part TV evangelists have no difficulty finding theological rationales for virulent anti-Sovietism and runaway militarism.

In the years ahead I think it is reasonable to expect that the interpretation of religion will continue to be debated on the public stage, both in Latin America and outside it—in the United States and Europe. There will be a public conflict over competing theologies whether they are called by that name or not. Such controversy is likely to continue as long as the underlying crises remain unresolved.

REFERENCES

CHAPTER 1–BIRTH PANGS: EMERGENCE OF LIBERATION THEOLOGY

On historical matters see Enrique Dussel, *A History of the Church in Latin America: Colonialism to Liberation (1492–1979)* (Grand Rapids, Mich.: William B. Eerdmans Publishing Company, 1981); and Pablo Richard, *Morte das Cristiandades e Nascimento da Igreja* (São Paulo: Paulinas, 1984; translation forthcoming from Orbis Books). On las Casas and the other bishops who defended the Indians, see Enrique Dussel, *El Episcopado Latinoamericano y la Liberación de los Pobres 1504–1620* (Mexico City: CRT [Centro de Reflexión Teológica], 1979), esp. pp. 325–34.

On Camilo Torres see Walter J. Broderick, *Camilo Torres: A Biography of the Priest-Guerrillero* (Garden City, N.Y.: Doubleday,

1975). Quote from "Mensaje a los Cristianos" in Camilo Torres, *Cristianismo y Revolución*, ed. Oscar Maldonado, Guitemie Oliviéri, and Germán Zabala (Mexico City: Ediciones Era, 1970), p. 525.

Paul VI quote: *Populorum Progressio*, in Joseph Gremillion, ed., *The Gospel of Peace and Justice* (Maryknoll, N.Y.: Orbis Books, 1976), p. 396.

Medellín documents: CELAM, *La Iglesia en la Actual Transformación de América Latina a la Luz del Concilio, Vol. II—Conclusiones* (Bogotá: CELAM, 1969), p. 43. (Henceforth cited as "Medellín.")

For a survey of the early phase of liberation theology: Phillip Berryman, "Latin American Liberation Theology," in Sergio Torres and John Eagleson, eds., *Theology in the Americas* (Maryknoll, N.Y.: Orbis Books, 1976), pp. 20–83. The article by Methol Ferre, "Iglesia y Sociedad Opulenta, Una Crítica a Suenens Desde América Latina," was a special supplement to the Uruguayan magazine *Víspera*.

On Christians for Socialism: John Eagleson, ed., *Christians and Socialism: Documentation of the Christians for Socialism Movement in Latin America* (Maryknoll, N.Y.: Orbis Books, 1975), esp. the final document, pp. 160–75; quote from p. 174.

CHAPTER 2 – GOING TO THE POOR

Beting remark: Frei Betto, *Fidel e a Religião: Conversas com Frei Betto* (São Paulo: Editora Brasiliense, 1985), p. 56.

On poverty as theological theme: Gustavo Gutiérrez, *A Theology of Liberation* (Maryknoll, N.Y.: Orbis Books, 1973), pp. 287ff. Quote from p. 300. Medellín quote, document on poverty, par. 5, p. 209.

Freire presents his ideas most systematically in *Pedagogy of the Op-*

pressed (New York: Herder & Herder, 1970), and *Education for Critical Consciousness* (New York: The Seabury Press, 1973).

For a sense of evangelization/*concientización* see Pastoral Team of Bambamarca, *Vamos Caminando: A Peruvian Catechism* (Maryknoll, N.Y.: Orbis Books, 1985). This book, which contains dozens of discussion outlines, is a fine example of this kind of pedagogy. Most lessons have a case study set within a fictionalized area of highlands Peru with suggestive questions for discussion. Some discussions begin with a Scripture passage.

Puebla document: John Eagleson and Philip Sharper, eds., *Puebla and Beyond: Documentation and Commentary*, trans. John Drury (Maryknoll, N.Y.: Orbis Books, 1979), pars. 28, 1209, 1134. (Henceforth cited as "Puebla.")

CHAPTER 3 – MIRROR OF LIFE: THE BIBLE READ BY THE POOR

Biblical quotations are adapted from the New American Bible.

Transcripts of several years of group biblical reflections by a group of fishing families and peasants together with the poet Ernesto Cardenal are found in Ernesto Cardenal, *The Gospel in Solentiname*, 4 vols. (Maryknoll, N.Y.: Orbis Books, 1982).

Prophecy: Jon Sobrino, *Monseñor Romero: Verdadero Profeta* (Managua: IHCA-CAV, 1981). Puebla, par. 267.

Frei Betto quote in Guillermo Cook, *The Expectation of the Poor: Latin American Basic Ecclesial Communities in Protestant Perspective* (Maryknoll, N.Y.: Orbis Books, 1985), p. 110.

The most systematic exposition of the principles of interpretation underlying liberation theology are found in Clodovis Boff, *Teologia e Prática: Teologia do Político e Suas Mediações* (Petrópolis, Brazil:

Vozes, 1978), esp. sec. 2, pp. 131–271. For a shorter treatment see J. Severino Croatto, "Biblical Hermeneutics in the Theologies of Liberation," in Virginia Fabella and Sergio Torres, eds., *Irruption of the Third World: Challenge to Theology* (Maryknoll, N.Y.: Orbis Books, 1983), pp. 140–70; and Croatto, *Exodus: A Hermeneutics of Freedom* (Maryknoll, N.Y.: Orbis Books, 1981).

CHAPTER 4 – A NEW MODEL OF CHURCH: CHRISTIAN BASE COMMUNITIES

The figures on numbers of base communities seem to be a rough estimation or even an extrapolation. There is a surprising dearth of research on base communities. In *Ecclesiogenesis: The Base Communities Reinvent the Church* (Maryknoll, N.Y.: Orbis Books, 1986) pp. 3ff., Leonardo Boff cites the incident in Barra do Piraí as their starting point. Scott Mainwaring, *The Catholic Church and Politics in Brazil, 1916–1982* (dissertation; publication forthcoming), says none of today's communities can be traced back further than approximately 1963. On base communities see Cook, *The Expectation of the Poor.*

Aguilares statistics: Salvador Carranza, "Aguilares, una Experiencia de Evangelización Rural Parroquial," *ECA,* nos. 348/349 (October-November 1977): 845; and UCA Editores, *Rutilio Grande: Mártir de la Evangelización Rural en El Salvadore* (San Salvador: UCA Editores, 1978), p. 75.

On *basismo* see Scott Mainwaring, "The Catholic Church, Popular Education, and Political Change in Brazil," *Journal of Interamerican Studies and World Affairs* 26, no. 1 (February 1984): 97–124.

On national meetings of base communities in Brazil, see Leonardo Boff, *Ecclesiogenesis,* pp. 35ff. See also J. B. Libanio, "Igreja: Povo Oprimodo que se Organiza para a Liberatação," *Revista Eclesiastica Brasileira* 41, fasc. 16 (June 1981) pp. 297–311; and Clodovis

Boff, "Crônica do V Encontro Intereclesial de Comunidades de Base (Canindé, CE, 04 a 08-07-1983)," *Revista Eclesiastica Brasileira* 43, fasc. 171 (September 1983) pp. 471–93.

On new missionary activity by base community members: Joseph Comblin, "O Novo Ministerio de Missionario na America Latina," in *Revista Eclesiastica Brasileira* 40, fasc. 160 (December 1980) pp. 626–55.

Puebla on base communities, pars. 261, 630.

CHAPTER 5 – FEET-ON-THE-GROUND: FROM EXPERIENCE TO THEOLOGY

Clodovis Boff's "theological journal": *Teologia Pê-No-Chão* (Petrópolis, Brazil: Vozes, 1984; translation forthcoming from Orbis Books). Methodology: *Teologia e Prática: Teologia do Político e Suas Mediações* (Petrópolis, Brazil: Vozes, 1978).

Sobrino essay: "Unity and Conflict in the Church" in Jon Sobrino, *The True Church and the Poor* (Maryknoll N.Y.: Orbis Books, 1984), pp. 194–227.

Segundo essay: "Two Theologies of Liberation," *The Month* (London), October 1984, pp. 321–27.

Boff distinctions on social science: *Teologia e Prática*, pp. 122ff. Quote of Leonardo Boff from Leonardo and Clodovis Boff, *Salvation and Liberation* (Maryknoll, N.Y.: Orbis Books, 1984), p. 50.

Prebisch quote is cited in Ronald H. Chilcote, *Theories of Development and Under-development* (Boulder, Colo.: Westview Press, 1984), p. 26. Chilcote's book provides a useful outline of the dependence discussion, as does his *Theories of Comparative Politics: The Search for a Paradigm* (Boulder, Colo.: Westview Press, 1981).

Segundo quote: Rosino Gibellini, ed., *Frontiers of Theology in Latin America* (Maryknoll, N.Y.: Orbis Books, 1979), pp. 249–50.

On Nicaraguan economic strategy: Michael E. Conroy, "Economic Legacy and Policies: Performance and Critique," in Thomas W. Walker, ed., *Nicaragua: The First Five Years* (New York: Praeger, 1985), pp. 219–44. For an important theoretical study see E. V. K. FitzGerald, "Planned Accumulation and Income Distribution in the Small Peripheral Economy," in George Irvin and Xabier Gorostiaga, eds., *Towards an Alternative for Central America and the Caribbean* (London: George Allen & Unwin, 1985), pp. 95–110. See also Joseph Collins, Frances Moore Lappé, and Nick Allen, *Nicaragua: What Difference Could a Revolution Make?*, rev. ed. (San Francisco: Institute for Food and Development Policy, 1985).

Populorum Progressio quote: Joseph Gremillion, ed., *The Gospel of Peace and Justice* (Maryknoll, N.Y.: Orbis Books), par. 21, p. 393 (translation slightly modified).

Gutiérrez quotes: Gutiérrez, *A Theology of Liberation*, pp. 36–37.

For a very illuminating comparison between liberation theology and "critical theory," see Joseph Kroger, "Prophetic-Critical and Practical-Strategic Tasks of Theology: Habermas and Liberation Theology," *Theological Studies* 46 (1985): 3–20.

CHAPTER 6 – CAPTIVITY AND HOPE: SHIFTING CONTEXTS OF LIBERATION THEOLOGY

The best account of the experience of the church during the 1970s is Penny Lernoux, *Cry of the People: The Struggle for Human Rights in Latin America—the Catholic Church in Conflict with U.S. Policy* (New York: Penguin, 1982). Enrique Dussel, *De Medellín a Puebla: Una Década de Sangre y Esperanza 1968–1979* (Mexico City: Edicol, 1979) gathers a great deal of valuable material.

Vekemans and the CIA: Lernoux, *Cry of the People*, p. 26. Statistics on murdered church people: Ibid., pp. 463ff.

"Banzer Plan": Ibid., pp. 142–47.

CHAPTER 7 – THE INFINITE WORTH OF THE POOR: A CRITICAL VISION OF HUMAN RIGHTS

Guatemalan bishops' quote: "Unidos en la Esperanza," in UCA Editores, *Los Obispos Latinoamericanos Entre Medellín y Puebla: Documentos Episcopales 1968–1979* (San Salvador: UCA Editores, 1978), p. 183. For a massive collection of episcopal statements cf. José Marins, Teolide M. Trevisán, and Carolee Chanoma, *Praxis de los Padres de América Latina: Los Documentos de las Conferencias Episcopales de Medellín a Puebla (1968–1978)* Bogotá: Paulinas, 1978).

DEI publications: Hugo Assmann, ed., *Carter y la Lógica del Imperialismo* 2 vols., (San José, Costa Rica: EDUCA, 1978); and Elsa Tamez and Saul Trinidad, eds., *Capitalismo: Violencia y Anti-Vida—La Opresión de las Mayorías y la Domesticación de los Dioses*, 2 vols. (San José, Costa Rica: EDUCA, 1978). Segundo essay in *Capitalismo*, vol. 2, pp. 339–53: quote from p. 348.

On the national security state: Bishop Cândido Padín, "A Doctrina da Segurança Nacional," *Revista Eclesiastica Brasileira* 37, fasc. 146 (June 1977) pp. 331–42. Joseph Comblin, *The Church and the National Security State*, passim, esp. chaps. 4–6; his theological critique of national security ideology is found on pp. 88ff. Puebla on national security ideology, pars. 314, 547, 1262.

Documents of bishops of northeastern and central western Brazil: UCA Editores, eds., *Los Obispos Latinoamericanos*, pp. 40ff. and 64ff; quotes on pp. 62, 71.

CHAPTER 8–TAKING SIDES: FAITH, POLITICS, AND IDEOLOGY

Vatican II quote: "Pastoral Constitution on the Church in the Modern World," in Walter M. Abbot, ed., *The Documents in Vatican II* (New York: America Press, 1966), par. 76, p. 287.

Paul VI: *Octogesima Adveniens,* in Gremillion, *The Gospel of Peace and Justice,* pars. 24–36, pp. 497–501. Puebla on politics, pars. 513–30.

On church and popular organizations: Phillip Berryman, *The Religious Roots of Rebellion: Christians in Central American Revolutions* (Maryknoll, N.Y.: Orbis Books, 1984), chaps. 4–6 and pp. 337ff.

Discussion of ideologies: The "Caracas theologians" remained anonymous presumably for security reasons and perhaps to avoid unnecessary problems with church authorities. The discussion of ideologies is to be found in *Iglesia Que Nace del Pueblo: Reflexiones y Problemas* (Mexico City: Centro de Reflexión Teológica, 1978), pp. 30ff. Puebla on ideologies, pars. 535ff.

Christendom discussion: Pablo Richard, *Morte das Cristiandades e Nascimento da Igreja: Analise Historica e Interpretação Teológica da Igreja na America Latina* (São Paulo: Paulinas, 1984). The original form is *Mort des Chrétientés et Naissance de l'Église* (Paris: Centre Lebret, 1978). His reflection on Nicaragua is found in "Identidad Eclesial en el Proceso Revolucionario," in CAV-IHCA (Centro Antonio Valdiviesco-Instituto Histórico Centroamericano), *Apuntes para una Teología Nicaragüense,* (Managua: CAV-IHCA, 1981), pp. 91–103. Comblin on christendom: *O Tempo da Ação: Ensaio sobre o Espírito e a História* (Petrópolis, Brazil: Vozes, 1982), chap. 4, "O Desafio da Cristiandade."

■ ■ ■

CHAPTER 9–UTILIZING MARXISM: OBSERVATIONS ON PRACTICE AND THEOLOGY

"Polite relationship" remark: Juan Luis Segundo, *Theology and the Church: A Response to Cardinal Ratzinger and a Warning to the Whole Church* (Minneapolis: Seabury-Winston, 1985), p. 91.

Use of Marxism: Caracas theologians, *Iglesia Que Nace del Pueblo,* pp. 42–59.

On the church in Nicaragua the literature is immense. See Berryman, *Religious Roots,* Chap. 8; and Michael Dodson and Laura Nuzzi O'Shaughnessy, "Religion and Politics," in Walker, ed., *Nicaragua: The First Five Years,* pp. 119–43. For a well-written attack on the Sandinistas and Christians who support the revolution, see Humberto Belli, *Breaking Faith: The Sandinista Revolution and its Impact on Freedom and Christian Faith in Nicaragua* (Garden City, Mich.: Puebla Institute, 1985). For the theological rationale for active Christian involvement, see Berryman, *Religious Roots*, passim, esp. pp. 354ff.; and Juan Hernandez Pico, "The Experience of Nicaragua's Revolutionary Christians," in Sergio Torres and John Eagleson, eds., *The Challenge of Basic Christian Communities* (Maryknoll, N.Y.: Orbis Books, 1981), pp. 62–73. See also IHCA, *Fe Cristiana y Revolución Sandinista en Nicaragua* (Managua: IHCA, 1979); IHCA-CAV, *Apuntes para una Teología Nicaragüense* (San José, Costa Rica: DEI, 1981); and the two works edited by Teofilo Cabestrero, *Ministers of God, Ministers of the People* (Maryknoll, N.Y.: Orbis Books, 1984) and *Revolutionaries for the Gospel: Testimonies of Fifteen Christians in the Nicaraguan Government* (Maryknoll, N.Y.: Orbis Books, 1986). For criticism of the revolution see IHCA-CAV, *Los Cristianos Interpelan a la Revolución: Fidelidad Crítica en el Proceso de Nicaragua* (Managua: IHCA-CAV, 1981). This short book has the text of the document prepared by the primarily middle-class Christians for the revolution that reflected on seven challenges, and the responses by Christians and Sandinistas at the conference following two months of grass-roots discussion.

Theologians dealing with Marxism: José Porfirio Miranda, *Marx and the Bible: A Critique of the Philosophy of Oppression* (Maryknoll, N.Y.: Orbis Books, 1974); *Communism in the Bible* (Maryknoll, N.Y.: Orbis Books, 1982); *Marx Against the Marxists* (Maryknoll, N.Y.: Orbis Books, 1980).

Fetishism: Franz Hinkelammert, *The Ideological Weapons of Death* (Maryknoll, N.Y.: Orbis Books, 1986). Hugo Assmann, "O Uso de Simbolos Biblicos em Marx," *Revista Eclesiastica Brasileira* 45, fasc. 178 (June 1985); quote from Assmann, p. 329.

CHAPTER 10–GOD OF LIFE: THE RELIGIOUS VISION OF LIBERATION THEOLOGY

On idolatry: See Pablo Richard et al., *The Battle of the Gods* (Maryknoll, N.Y.: Orbis Books, 1984), esp. Jon Sobrino, "The Epiphany of the God of Life in Jesus Christ," pp. 66–102. Sobrino expresses similar ideas on transcendence in "Dios y los Procesos Revolucionarios," in CAV-IHCA, *Apuntes para una Teología Nicaragüense*, pp. 105–29.

Church and kingdom: Virtually all theologians deal with this theme. It is a unifying point of the essays of Ignacio Ellacuría collected in *Conversión de la Iglesia al Reino de Dios: Para Anunciarlo y Realizarlo en la Historia* (San Salvador: UCA Editores, 1985).

Sobrino quote: "The Witness of the Church in Latin America," in Torres and Eagleson, eds., *The Challenge of Basic Christian Communities*, p. 166.

▪ ▪ ▪

CHAPTER 11–OTHER ACCENTS: THIRD WORLD, BLACK, HISPANIC, AND FEMINIST THEOLOGIES

Third World theological dialogue is documented in volumes emerging from conferences of EATWOT (Ecumenical Association of Third World Theologians), all published by Orbis Books: Sergio Torres and Virginia Fabella, eds., *The Emergent Gospel: Theology from the Underside of History* (1978); Kofi Appiah-Kubi and Sergio Torres, eds., *African Theology En Route* (1978); Virginia Fabella, ed., *Asia's Struggle for a Full Humanity* (1980); Sergio Torres and John Eagleson, eds., *The Challenge of Basic Christian Communities* (1981); Virginia Fabella and Sergio Torres, eds., *Irruption of the Third World: Challenge to Theology* (1983); and Fabella and Torres, eds., *Doing Theology in a Divided World* (1985). "Irruption" passage from Fabella and Torres, eds., *Irruption*, p. 195.

Minjung theology: Fabella and Torres, eds., *Irruption*, p. 70.

Tissa Balasuriya, *Planetary Theology* (Maryknoll, N.Y.: Orbis Books, 1984).

Pieris essays: "Towards an Asian Theology of Liberation: Some Religio-Cultural Guidelines," in Fabella, eds., *Asia's Struggle*, pp. 75–95; and "The Place of Non-Christian Religions and Cultures in the Evolution of Third World Theology," in Fabella and Torres, eds., *Irruption*, pp. 113–39.

Black theology: Many documents and essays are collected in Gayraud S. Wilmore and James H. Cone, eds., *Black Theology: A Documentary History, 1966–1979* (Maryknoll, N.Y.: Orbis Books, 1979). *For My People: Black Theology and the Black Church* (Maryknoll, N.Y.: Orbis Books, 1984) represents a recent statement of James Cone's positions. Quote from Wilmore and Cone, eds., *Black Theology*, p. 101. See also Allan Aubrey Boesak, *Farewell to Innocence: A Socio-Ethical Study on Black Theology and Power* (Maryknoll, N.Y.: Orbis Books, 1977).

Hispanic church and theology: Antonio M. Arroyo, ed., *Prophets Denied Honor: An Anthology on the Hispanic Church in the United States* (Maryknoll, N.Y.: Orbis Books, 1980). Virgilio Elizondo, *Galilean Journey: The Mexican-American Promise* (Maryknoll, N.Y.: Orbis Books, 1983).

Feminist theology: Cora Ferro, "The Latin American Woman: The Praxis and Theology of Liberation," in Torres and Eagleson, eds., *The Challenge*, pp. 24–37; quote from p. 33. Elisabeth Schüssler-Fiorenza, " 'You Are Not to Be Called Father': Early Christian History in a Feminist Perspective," and Luise Schottroff, "Women as Followers of Jesus in New Testament Times: An Exercise in Social-Historical Exegesis of the Bible," both in Norman K. Gottwald, ed., *The Bible and Liberation: Political and Social Hermeneutics* (Maryknoll, N.Y.: Orbis Books, 1983), pp. 394–417, 418–27. Rosemary Radford Ruether, *Sexism and God-Talk: Toward a Feminist Theology* (Boston: Beacon Press, 1983), esp. pp. 61, 66, 85, 138, 232–33, 254, 257.

CHAPTER 12 – DOES IT LIBERATE? OBJECTIONS TO LIBERATION THEOLOGY

Critiques of liberation theology: CELAM, *Liberación: Diálogos en el CELAM* (Bogotá: Secretariado General del CELAM, 1974). The contributions of López Trujillo, Poblete, and Kloppenburg summarize the main objections well. James V. Schall, ed., *Liberation Theology in Latin America* (San Francisco: Ignatius Press, 1982) is also a good summary. Gerard Berghoef and Lester DeKoster, *Liberation Theology: The Church's Future Shock—Explanation, Analysis, Critique, Alternative*, provides an evangelical critique. Michael Novak argues his position in, "The Case Against Liberation Theology," *New York Times Magazine*, October 21, 1984; p. 51ff.; *The Spirit of Democratic Capitalism* (New York: Simon & Schuster, 1982), esp. pp. 272–314; *Freedom with Justice: Catholic Social*

Thought and Liberal Institutions (San Francisco: Harper & Row, 1984), esp. pp. 183–94.

Wolf reference: Eric R. Wolf, *Europe and the People Without History* (Berkeley: University of California Press, 1982). Ramos' essays "Reflections on Gustavo Gutiérrez's Theology of Liberation," "Dependency and Development: An Attempt to Clarify the Issues," "On the Prospects for Social Market Democracy—or Democratic Capitalism—in Latin America," and "Latin America: The End of Democratic Reformism?" as well as Sergio Molina and Sebastian Piñera, "Extreme Poverty in Latin America," are found in Michael Novak, ed., *Liberation South, Liberation North* (Washington, D.C.: American Enterprise Institute, 1981). Novak quote from *The Spirit of Democratic Capitalism*, p. 278.

Physical quality of life index: Morris David Morris, *Measuring the Condition of the World's Poor: The Physical Quality of Life Index* (New York: Pergamon Press, 1979), esp. data on pp. 130–32.

On Cuba: Claes Brundenius, "Development Strategies and Basic Needs in Revolutionary Cuba," in Claes Brundenius and Mats Lundahl, eds., *Development Strategies and Basic Needs in Latin America: Challenges for the 1980s* (Boulder, Colo.: Westview Press, 1982), p. 156. For data comparing Brazil, Peru, and Cuba, see table, p. 156. See also Joseph Collins and Medea Benjamin, *No Free Lunch: Food and Agriculture Policy in Cuba* (San Francisco: Institute for Food and Development Policy, 1983).

Ratzinger letter: The instruction itself is found in the *National Catholic Reporter*, September 21, 1984; references follow paragraphing. Juan Luis Segundo, *Theology and the Church: A Response to Cardinal Ratzinger and a Warning to the Whole Church* (Minneapolis: Seabury-Winston, 1985).

▪ ▪ ▪

CHAPTER 13–LOOKING AHEAD

U.S. Catholic bishops' pastoral letters: "The Challenge of Peace," in *Origins* 13, no. 1 (May 19, 1983): 4. Second draft of "Pastoral Letter on Catholic Social Teaching and the U.S. Economy" (October 7, 1985), par. 46, p. 14.

INDEX

About the Author

Phillip Berryman was a priest in a barrio in Panama during 1965–73, the years in which the new liberation theology and pastoral practice in Latin America were taking shape. From 1976 to 1980, as Central American representative for the American Friends Service Committee, he was in a privileged position to observe the deepening crisis in the region. In 1980, he returned from Guatemala to the United States and now lives in Philadelphia with his wife and three daughters, continuing to do research and writing. He has published numerous reviews and articles in such journals as *Commonweal*, *America*, and *The National Catholic Reporter*, and is the author of *The Religious Roots of Rebellion* and *Inside Central America*.